THE PERMANENT COURT OF ARBITRATION
PEACE PALACE PAPERS

PCA International Law Seminar
December 9, 1999

The Permanent Court of Arbitration/Peace Palace Papers

INSTITUTIONAL AND PROCEDURAL ASPECTS OF MASS CLAIMS SETTLEMENT SYSTEMS

Papers emanating from the PCA International Law Seminar
on December 9, 1999

Inaugural Seminar

Edited by
The International Bureau of the
Permanent Court of Arbitration

KLUWER LAW INTERNATIONAL
The Hague/London/Boston

Published by:
Kluwer Law International
P.O. Box 85889, 2508 CN The Hague, The Netherlands
sales@kli.wkap.nl
http://www.kluwerlaw.com

Sold and Distributed in North, Central and South America by:
Kluwer Law International
657 Massachusetts Avenue, Cambridge, MA 02139, USA

Sold and Distributed in all other countries by:
Kluwer Law International
Distribution Centre, P.O. Box 322, 3300 AH Dordrecht, The Netherlands

A C.I.P. Catalogue record for this book is available from the Library of Congress

Printed on acid-free paper.

ISBN 90 411 1406 8

Kluwer Law International incorporates the publishing programmes
of Graham & Trotman Ltd, Kluwer Law and Taxation Publishers
and Martinus Nijhoff Publishers

TABLE OF CONTENTS

OTHER RELATED ARTICLES

ANNEXES 73

INTRODUCTION

*Tjaco T. van den Hout**

On November 15, 1999, at its 54th session, the United Nations General Assembly reiterated the importance of the role of the Permanent Court of Arbitration (PCA) in the field of international dispute settlement and invited States to consider making greater use of PCA's facilities and to support its work.[1] This work also encompasses the promotion of a wider appreciation of international law in general and of the science of arbitration in particular, *inter alia*, through the holding of symposia, conferences and seminars, and the publication of books and other materials. Earlier in the year, the Second Conference of the Members of the Permanent Court of Arbitration, meeting in the Peace Palace in The Hague on May 17, 1999, on the occasion of the celebration of the centenary of the Court, singled out such activities as deserving of greater support.[2]

I am pleased that, with the above expressions by the international community in mind, at the close of the United Nations Decade of International Law as well as of our Centennial, we were able to launch a new series of semi-annual seminars each of which will be followed by a publication of the seminar's papers, to be known as *The PCA/Peace Palace Papers*. The inaugural seminar was devoted to a subject of great topical interest: institutional and procedural aspects of mass claims settlement systems. The proceedings have been compiled in the present volume, together with supplementary commentary. Operational issues pertaining to mass claims settlement systems are of immediate relevance not only to claimants and their attorneys but also to governments. Apart from the informative value of this volume for interested parties, this seminar and the publication of its proceedings are also important for the PCA itself as this constitutes a first step on the road to realizing its goal of becoming: a full-fledged "documentation center" for mass claims settlement systems – a role originally

* Secretary-General, Permanent Court of Arbitration; formerly Deputy Secretary-General, Netherlands Ministry of Foreign Affairs; JD, Leyden University (1973).

1. Doc. A/54/609, United Nations Decade of International Law.
2. Res. 17 May 1999, oper. para. 8.

proposed by Judge Howard Holtzmann at the PCA Members' Conference in May 1999. Such a role would fall quite naturally to the PCA in the light of its past and present involvement with the Iran-United States Claims Tribunal,[3] considered by many as one of the most important and innovative mass claims systems ever established.

This volume compiles the contributions of the panelists who shared with us their experience with major mass claims systems currently in operation from the vantage point of their respective roles in those systems, i.e., as arbitrator, counsel or administrator. Other relevant material has been added to the volume to complement the original input. The whole has been enriched by a comprehensive Overview, prepared by Judge Howard Holtzmann. I am, of course, indebted to him and the panelists for their efforts to help realize this publication.

International claims settlement mechanisms, it is said, can only be successful if they offer recourse to a wide range of legal norms. The Iran-United States Claims Tribunal is conveniently used as a point of reference, as it has proven to be a system able to use a variety of legal norms, ranging from contract provisions and municipal law to principles of international commercial usage (*lex mercatoria*) and principles of public international law.[4] However, the more recent claims systems, such as the UN Compensation Commission, the Commission for Real Property Claims in Bosnia and Herzegovina and the Claims Resolution Tribunal for Dormant Accounts in Switzerland, defy that notion in one way or another. This is due in large part to the institutional and procedural arrangements applicable to those systems.

The United Nations Compensation Commission (UNCC) has been coined "a curious creation from an institutional point of view, assuming the form of a hybrid between an administrative claims procedure and an international tribunal". Compared to the Iran-US Claims Tribunal, the UNCC possesses a

---

3. See, George H. Aldrich, "The Iran-United States Claims Tribunal", *The Permanent Court of Arbitration: International Arbitration and Dispute Resolution* (Kluwer Law International 1999) pp. 206-245.
4. D. Bederman, "Historic Analogues of the UN Compensation Commission", Lillich, Ed., *The United Nations Compensation Commission: Thirteenth Sokol Colloquium*.

structure and procedure very different to that of an adjudicative body.[5] However, whatever difficulties some might have with the institutional model chosen, it is a remarkable example of the settlement of claims in the aftermath of war. Its decisions are expected to "have significance to future international trade, and to shaping future tribunals for resolving business dispute arising out of public international conflicts".[6]

The Claims Resolution Tribunal for Dormant Accounts in Switzerland (CRT) is yet again very different, due to the *sui generis* nature of the problem of dormant bank accounts. The CRT is "undoubtedly a unique institution and many of its problems are peculiar to it and to the process that has been imposed upon it". However, for the insurance and art tribunals that are currently envisioned, there is a wealth of experience to be gained from the operations of the CRT.[7]

One of the papers in this volume deals with institutional and procedural aspects of mass claims litigation and settlement in two cases of environmental disasters. After damage caused by diplomatic crises and wars, environmental damage is the obvious second area deserving of orderly recourse to compensation. Recent environmental disasters affecting rivers in the Carpathian Basin in Central Europe give added urgency to the need to seek environmental protection through provisions in the appropriate legal instruments and other arrangements (e.g., investment agreements).

The various papers in this volume offer a unique insight to students, practitioners and policy makers in the mechanics of the systems, individually and taken together. I trust the reader will find this publication useful both in terms of content, as well as format, the latter having been adopted to facilitate comparison among systems.

---

5. Hans Wassgren, "The UN Compensation Commission: Lessons in Legitimacy, State Responsibility, and War Reparations", 11 Leiden Journal of International Law (1998) pp. 473-492.
6. William E. Huth, "The Iraq Claims Tribunal: An Overview of the UN Compensation Commission", Dispute Resolution Journal (May 1999) pp. 25-31, 82-85.
7. Suzannah Linton, "Righting a Wrong or Prolonging the Agony? The Work of the Claims Resolution Tribunal for Dormant Accounts in Switzerland", 12 Leiden Journal of International Law (1999) pp. 373-389.

It is hoped that this "first step" has laid the foundation for further endeavors of the International Bureau in this field.

Mass Claims Settlement Systems: Potentials and Pitfalls

*Howard M. Holtzmann**

The papers collected in this book describe the practical experience of various tribunals and legal systems in resolving large numbers of claims arising from common circumstances. Four of the papers analyze special arbitral – or, perhaps, quasi-arbitral – tribunals that were established to resolve large numbers of claims arising from highly contentious historic events. The fifth paper discusses proceedings in national courts for deciding mass claims resulting from two man-made disasters.

The first of the modern claims systems was the Iran-United States Claims Tribunal created in The Hague in 1981 to resolve thousands of claims resulting from the Islamic Revolution in Iran. It was followed by the United Nations Compensation Commission in Geneva to resolve millions of claims related to the Gulf War. Then came the Commission for Property Claims in Bosnia and Herzegovina to deal with losses suffered by hundreds of thousands of individuals displaced from their homes. More recently, the Claims Resolution Tribunal for Dormant Accounts in Switzerland was formed to decide thousands of claims arising from the Holocaust. In contrast to these four special tribunals, thousands of claims were submitted to national courts in the United States and India arising after an oil spill from the tanker Exxon Valdez that ran aground on the Alaskan coast and a gas leak from a chemical plant in Bhopal, India.

The most striking lesson to be derived from these five valuable papers is that special tribunals are more appropriate for resolving mass claims than are national courts. That is because, as the first four papers show, creating a special tribunal offers the potential for flexibility to design procedures and institutional arrangements in the light of the particular nature of the claims and any unique circumstances that may be involved. Moreover, special tribunals can be truly international, thus offering the potential for wider accept-

* Member, Iran-United States Claims Tribunal, 1981-1994, *ad hoc* Member 1994- ; Member, Claims Resolution Tribunal for Dormant Accounts in Switzerland, 1998- .

ability of their decisions. Those advantages of special tribunals contrast sharply with the rigidity of formal procedures that must be faced even in relatively enlightened national court systems. In view of the emerging potential of special tribunals, I will focus this discussion on them rather than on proceedings in national courts.

A further lesson of these papers is that the establishment of a special tribunal can be a valuable – indeed, often an indispensable – element in settling difficult diplomatic disputes. That same potential benefit motivated the drafters of the 1899 Hague Convention for the Settlement of International Disputes which anticipated use of special tribunals to resolve political disputes and it continues to have practical validity today. Thus, each of the special tribunals described in this book was created in the context of a political crisis.

We must, however, candidly recognize that the potential benefits of special tribunals are accompanied by a number of possible pitfalls that can threaten the success of the process. While the circumstances that led to the establishment of the four tribunals described in these papers were very different and their structures are widely varied, nonetheless a comparative study of their experiences can provide lessons for each other and also for new tribunals that may be needed in the future. Such analyses can help to realize the potentials and to avoid the pitfalls.

Some examples of topics for comparative study suggested by the experience of the four tribunals are outlined below. The order in which these topics are mentioned does not indicate my view of their relative importance, for I consider that all of them require careful attention. Moreover, these topics are illustrative examples and do not constitute an exclusive list because further examination is likely to reveal additional subjects for comparative analysis.

I. BALANCING ARBITRAL AND ADMINISTRATIVE APPROACHES

Dr. Norbert Wühler cogently points out in his paper on the UN Compensation Commission that "in every mass claims programme a tension exists . . . between the search for individual justice and fairness and the requirement of an expedient process that resolves all the claims within a reasonable time period." In practical terms, the designers of special tribunals seek to find a balance between procedures that are akin to typical arbitration and those that favor an administrative approach. When doing so, the roles of arbitrators and administrators must be carefully defined and understood in order to prevent confusion and frustration. Comparative study of the four tribunals can help illuminate that central issue.

II. DRAFTING RULES OF PROCEDURE

As Ms. Lucy Reed states in her paper on the Iran-United States Claims Tribunal, "I cannot emphasize enough how important it was that the Tribunal started with a suitable and clear set of procedural rules." At that tribunal the rules are based on the widely-accepted UNCITRAL Arbitration Rules, while the three other special tribunals invented their own rules, departing in varying degrees from typical arbitration rules. Those variations may be seen to reflect the differences between predominately arbitral and largely administrative systems. Whatever the approach, the rules should be consistent with it. A comparative study of rules would be useful, including consideration of whether it is more effective for rules to be drafted by tribunal members who are often experienced arbitrators, or for rules to be handed down by others.

III. ESTABLISHING STANDARDS OF PROOF

All four of the special tribunals operate in circumstances in which claimants are unable to submit much of the evidence that would normally be needed to decide claims. For example, Prof. Hans van Houtte points out in his paper on the Commission for Real Property Claims in Bosnia and Herzegovina that large numbers of the official "property books" in which rights to real property were recorded were "destroyed [by force] before or during the war and many other records were taken away or tampered with." Similarly, Ms. Reed notes that the rules of the Claims Resolution Tribunal for Dormant Accounts in Switzerland establish a "relaxed" standard of proof and include a provision that arbitrators shall "at all times bear in mind the difficulty of proving a claim after the destruction of the Second World War and the Holocaust and the long time that has lapsed." The other special tribunals face similar problems. The different ways found to establish standards of proof are a fruitful field for analysis.

IV. FUNDING THE PROCESS

The methods of budgeting and the sources for financing the special tribunals differ. In some circumstances it is appropriate for one side to pay all of the costs of operating the tribunal. Regardless, however, of the source of funds, it is important that one side not have, or appear to have, a controlling or disproportionate influence on the budget. For decisions on how much a tribunal should spend and for what purposes, can affect the process and, consequently, the quality of justice. It would be interesting to see how sensitive the different tribunals have been to this problem and how effective they are in avoiding pitfalls related to it.

V. DEFINING THE FUNCTIONS OF THE ARBITRATORS AND THE SECRETARIAT

The roles of arbitrators (sometimes called "commissioners") and the secretariat differ in the various special tribunals. Pitfalls can be deep and dangerous if these roles are not carefully defined and fully understood by all concerned, particularly in areas in which the functions of the arbitrators and the secretariat overlap. Thus, the relationship between the arbitrators and the secretariat poses critical questions.

For example, should the arbitrators choose the secretariat, determine its functions, and supervise its activities, or should that be done solely by others? If that is to be done by the parties, what happens if after initial formation of the tribunal the parties disagree or delay acting? If such a situation occurs, should there be a fail-safe arrangement so that the tribunal can nevertheless move forward effectively?

All four tribunals recognize the need to provide legal assistance for arbitrators faced with thousands of claims. But that raises a number of practical questions. For example, does a legal staff chosen, assigned and supervised by the secretariat prepare drafts of procedural orders and awards, or is that done by assistants chosen by, and reporting to, each arbitrator? Is the work organized so that the arbitrators have sufficient opportunity to review and revise drafts, or would that slow the process and render it less efficient?

Recognizing that the secretariat has the task of furnishing staff and facilities, should the arbitrators exercise any oversight in these matters?

In posing these questions, I do not imply that there are any preferred or perfect answers. My purpose is simply to point out that answers to these, as well as other questions that can be identified by studying the experiences of various tribunals, should be analyzed and understood. That is necessary in order to achieve a smoothly operating process. This is another aspect in which comparative study could be useful.

VI. UNDERSTANDING THE ROLE OF COUNSEL

Ms. Reed in her paper on the Claims Resolution Tribunal for Dormant Bank Accounts in Switzerland discusses the role of counsel to represent the parties. She points out that "equality of representation, and good representation, assists the arbitrators and assists the arbitration process." In practice, the situation with respect to representation of all parties by counsel differs at the various special tribunals. As the papers in this book indicate, in one tribunal representation of all parties by counsel is the norm, while elsewhere it is effectively prohibited. In one of the special tribunals while counsel are not prohibited, one side is typically represented by counsel while the other side is not. In at least one of the tribunals, a mechanism was established to provide representation for claimants. In this context, questions arise as to whether representation by counsel is as necessary when the tribunal process is predominately administrative as compared with being more arbitral in nature. Arrangements assuring the availability of counsel are closely related to what in some systems is called "due process of law" and elsewhere is known as "natural justice" or is discussed under the rubric of "public policy." The different ways in which various special tribunals have dealt with these questions in different types of cases should be analyzed in order to avoid two kinds of pitfalls: (i) the danger that the process is not seen as being fair and equal, (ii) the difficulty that arbitrators encounter when they must decide complex issues without the benefit of the views of advocates for all sides.

VII. UTILIZING COMPUTER TECHNOLOGY

The papers in this book indicate the extent to which modern computer technology is used in the special tribunals and by the courts in organizing and expediting mass claims. The methods used include computerized databases and development of templates for use in preparing recurrent types of correspondence, procedural orders and awards. For example, Mr. Wühler, describing the UN Compensation Commission has reported that "for the assessment of thousands of small identical claims, this led to the use of sampling, statistical modelling and computerized matching for the verification and evaluation of the claims." Gathering and sharing information concerning the technologies developed by each of the special tribunals could increase the efficiency of the others and of future processes.

* * *

In sum, it is readily apparent that comparative study would contribute significantly to improving systems for the settlement of mass claims. But who will undertake that task and how will the results be made available? In that connection, I venture to repeat suggestions that I made in a keynote address at the Centennial celebration of the Permanent Court of Arbitration on May 17, 1999. Speaking of the four special tribunals that are the subject of the papers in this book, I said:

> "One thing is clear: there is no international arbitral institution where information concerning all of these mass claims processes is being collected, analyzed and compared by specialists in alternative dispute resolution. The PCA International Bureau is well equipped to fill this gap.
>
> As a first concrete step, the PCA might convene a meeting of individuals who have each been active in two or more of the mass claims processes that I have mentioned, either as arbitrators, administrators or counsel. An informal census indicates that there are [a number of persons] who have served at both The Hague and Geneva Tribunals and [others] who have participated in both The Hague and Zurich Tribunals and at least one who has served in The Hague, Geneva and Zurich Tribunals. Their experience is unique and their expertise is unparalleled. Working together, and with a few other experts, they might constitute a steering committee to recommend how the PCA could use its skills and facilities to assist in this complex field.
>
> One project might be to determine whether it would be useful for the PCA to collect relevant materials so that existing mass claims tribunals could benefit from the experience of others, and so that those who design future tribunals would have an easily

accessible source of useful information. Consideration might also be given to the types of support the PCA might offer to future mass claims tribunals, either as an administrator or a consultant.

I suggest that if the PCA undertakes this new task it should do so promptly, while data can still be found in current files before being relegated to dusty archives, and while individuals who have first-hand knowledge are readily available."

The seminar at which the papers in this book were presented created a significant foundation for such future action. The challenge is real. The tools are at hand. Let us proceed with the next steps.

Institutional and Procedural Aspects of Mass Claims Settlement Systems: The Iran-United States Claims Tribunal

*Lucy Reed**

Your Excellencies, Ladies and Gentlemen:

It is fitting that I am addressing you on the topic of procedural and institutional aspects of the Iran-United States Claims Tribunal in the Peace Palace as – many do not know or have forgotten – this is where it began.

As a young associate with my first law firm, I arrived in The Hague in the early morning hours of January 17, 1982. I was alone, but for some 25 or so boxes containing 20 copies each of some 30 Statements of Claim (per Note 2 to Art. 2 of the Tribunal Rules of Procedure[1]).

Shortly thereafter I filed those Claims in the temporary Registry here in the Peace Palace. I still remember the gracious and efficient assistance of Mr. Varekamp and others, who at least pretended not to be taken aback by the sheer quantity of paper in my custody.

Many times thereafter, both as counsel for private parties and as Agent for the United States Government from 1989 to 1992, I participated in Full Tribunal hearings in the small courtroom (the Tribunal's hearing rooms were too small). The assistance provided the Tribunal by the Permanent Court of Arbitration and the Carnegie Foundation is but one example of the institutional flexibility I will speak about in a few moments.

* Freshfields (New York).

1. *Editorial Note:* The Consolidated Tribunal Rules of Procedure of March 7, 1984, are reproduced as Annex I at pp. 75-106.

I. BACKGROUND ON THE TRIBUNAL AND STATUS REPORT

First, I would like to give some brief background on the Tribunal, recognizing that some in the audience may not be familiar with it.

The Tribunal was set up as part of the resolution in January 1981 of the protracted Iranian hostage crisis. This resolution was memorialized in two Declarations by the Government of Algeria, adhered to by the United States and Iran, which are known as the "Algiers Accords". The General Declaration set forth the terms for release of the hostages, and the Claims Settlement Declaration provided for establishment of the Tribunal to settle various categories of claims.

The Tribunal followed the pattern of earlier mixed international arbitral tribunals. There are nine arbitrators: three appointed by Iran, three appointed by the United States, and three others from third countries, who are appointed by the Government-appointed arbitrators or by the appointing authority, who is appointed by the Secretary-General of the Permanent Court of Arbitration. Most claims are decided in one of the three chambers, each consisting of a US, an Iranian and a third-country arbitrator. The Full Tribunal decides questions of interpretation of the Algiers Accords.

The Accords allowed US claimants seeking $250,000 or more ("large claims") to present their own claims through their own counsel, rather than rely on espousal by the US Government. Claims of less than $250,000 ("small claims") and disputes between the two Governments were handled by lawyers from the Office of International Claims and Investment Disputes of the State Department's Legal Adviser's Office. Iran relied both upon government lawyers, based in the Bureau for International Legal Services (BILS), and outside lawyers.

The Tribunal's jurisdiction is defined in Art. II of the Claims Settlement Declaration. Most important from a procedural standpoint, Sect. 2 grants jurisdiction over certain "official claims of the United States and Iran against each other" and Sect. 1 empowers the Tribunal to decide "claims of nationals of the United States against Iran and claims of nationals of Iran against the United States, and any counterclaim which arises out of the same contract, transaction or occurrence that constitutes the subject matter of that national's claim," arising "out of debts, contracts . . . expropriations or other measures affecting property rights . . .".

Art. II also specifies permissible claimants. The largest group, by far, were the hundreds of US companies and thousands of US individuals who left Iran after the Iranian revolution and taking of the hostages. The Tribunal was viable for these claimants primarily because, as part of the resolution of the hostage crisis, one billion dollars of previously frozen Iranian assets was escrowed to satisfy Tribunal awards.

Second, let me relay the extraordinary achievements of the Tribunal. More than 4,000 claims were filed. As of mid-1998 (when I last personally looked at statistics), the Tribunal had finalized 3,920 cases by award, decision or order (including the agreed lump-sum settlement of 2,388 "small claims"). In so doing, the Tribunal had awarded almost three billion dollars; issued 335 contested awards, 251 awards on agreed terms, 81 interim and interlocutory awards, and 129 decisions; issued over 20,000 orders; held 469 hearings and prehearing conferences; and dealt with almost 30,000 documents (of between one and 40 volumes) from the parties in almost 600,000 copies (Art. 2, Note 2 again). The Tribunal continues today with the small, but difficult, remaining caseload.

Clearly, these achievements rest upon strong procedural and institutional order. The Tribunal broke new ground in the procedural and institutional aspects of mass claims settlement systems. The lessons learned – both positive and negative – in connection with Tribunal procedure and administration fortunately have inured to the benefit of subsequent mass claims systems.

As perhaps the veteran in the group – at least as to the institutions represented – I particularly look forward to hearing from the representatives of some of those systems. Accordingly, I will limit my remarks tonight to three topics. I will address, first, the importance of the Tribunal's procedural rules and, second, the importance of publication of Tribunal awards. Third, I will list what I consider to be the most positive institutional aspects of the Tribunal.

As I prepared this, I was surprised again at how the most important procedural and institutional aspects are so fundamentally simple and basic. In essence, they are:

1. clear procedural rules tailored by those who will use them;

2. transparency as to procedures and outcome (but not, of course, deliberations);

3. organization, engineered to the needs of the parties involved.

II. TRIBUNAL RULES OF PROCEDURE

First, the Tribunal Rules of Procedure – the backbone of the entire process. I cannot emphasize enough how important it was that the Tribunal started with a suitable and clear set of procedural rules.

The Algiers Accords specified the UNCITRAL Arbitration Rules, which were still relatively new in 1981. After an exhaustive review by the judges, which confirmed the fit between those Rules and the Tribunal's largely commercial caseload, the judges adopted the UNCITRAL Rules with only minor modifications.

The beauty of the UNCITRAL Rules, as adopted by the Tribunal, is that they provide procedures that are both certain and flexible at the same time.

In a mass claims situation, the many claimants (and respondents) need to know – early on – exactly what to do, how to do it, and when to do it and where to do it, or there is chaos. This applies not just to filing procedures (e.g., Art. 2, Note 2, the number of copies) but also to major matters such as arbitrator replacement procedures. There is no room, with so many parties, for uncertainty.

Equally, because mass claims are rarely identical claims, there is no room for inflexibility. The Tribunal deftly used the flexibility built into the UNCITRAL Rules, for example, to tailor its hearings to the needs of vastly different cases: from multi-hundred million dollar oil expropriation cases with hordes of counsel and experts, to minor sale contract cases with *pro se* claimants. As a result, each Tribunal case felt more like a separate international commercial arbitration than another case on a court docket.

Those of us who practice international commercial arbitration have reaped the benefits of the "UNCITRAL Rule jurisprudence" developed by the Tribunal. So has the United Nations Compensation Commission (UNCC), and so will future mass claims systems.

III. PUBLICATION OF TRIBUNAL AWARDS

We would not have reaped these benefits, however many cases decided, if the Tribunal had not published its awards. This takes me to my second topic.

Publication, or transparency if you will, seems like a simple matter now. It was controversial for the Tribunal, and likely will be revisited with each multiple claims arbitration institution, given the arbitral culture of confidentiality.

Much has been written about the invaluable contribution to international law of the substantive Tribunal jurisprudence – as I mentioned, the publication of more than 350 reasoned awards in contested cases, to which we all have access. Far less glamorous are the benefits of publication to procedure, a few of which I will highlight here.

First, speaking from my perspective as US Agent assisting literally hundreds of US claimants and their counsel, the availability of procedural precedents allowed parties to write better memorials and conduct better hearings. It is easy to forget now how intimidating and confusing a Tribunal case could seem to the uninitiated – and most were uninitiated. Precedents, as well as word-of-mouth in the claimant community, provided a road map.

Second, publication facilitated settlements, which takes on great importance in mass claims situations. It was certainly Tribunal precedent that allowed the Governments to agree the lump-sum settlement of the 2,300-plus "small claims," which were mostly claims of individual everyday US nationals with losses in Iran. Unfortunately, despite a test case approach, this did not occur until 1990. Fortunately, in part because of our experience at the Tribunal, the UNCC was able to do far better for its small individual claimants, as you will likely hear from Dr. Norbert Wühler.

Third, publication demonstrated that, in a mass claims institution as in a national court, transparency is its own reward. All my experience with the Tribunal, both in my private and public roles, reinforced my belief that transparency promotes accountability which promotes due process for the parties.

IV. THE MOST POSITIVE INSTITUTIONAL ASPECTS OF THE TRIBUNAL

Let me turn now from procedural to institutional aspects of the Tribunal, my third and final topic.

To open, a disclosure: my perspective on the most positive aspects of the Tribunal as an institution is definitely colored by my subsequent experiences advising on the setting up of the UNCC and the Claims Resolution Tribunal for Dormant Swiss Bank Accounts in Switzerland.[2] Certain institutional aspects of the Tribunal that I discounted, or did not even notice, now seem quite significant.

I can touch upon only a few of the most positive institutional aspects of the Tribunal. In no particular order:

First, where a mass claims court is established, it is important to the parties to have actual physical aspects of seriousness and solidity. The Tribunal (after its temporary start in the Peace Palace) had its own building, with administrative systems, security, good working space, and a long-term staff.

Second, the Tribunal had full-time resident Agents from the US and Iranian Governments. This allowed the Governments best to protect, or at least advocate, their rights and exercise their responsibilities as sponsors and funders. In the case of the United States, the Agent was able to represent the interests of the private US claimant community in specific cases (i.e., by attending all hearings, and occasionally reminding the panels of procedural precedents) and in general (i.e., by urging expedition). My experience as Agent has colored my world view, putting primary emphasis on the interest of the claimant community – or, more broadly, both sets of parties.

Third, the Tribunal had full-time resident judges, with full-time legal assistants. I well-recognize that many of the best international arbitrators cannot make themselves available full-time for a period of several years, but I firmly believe that the magnitude and nature of the Tribunal caseload justified the Governments in demanding this commitment.

---

2. *Editorial Note:* For the article by Ms. Reed on the Claims Resolution Tribunal for Dormant Swiss Bank Accounts in Switzerland, see pp. 59-72.

Fourth, the Tribunal employed experienced administrative professionals: interpreters, translators, registrars, and secretaries. Although there is always the risk of bureaucratization, the comparatively low turnover benefited the claimant community and the Governments.

Fifth, the Chamber system – one Iranian, one US, and one third-country arbitrator sitting as a Chamber – facilitated the melding of procedures from the United States common law, Iranian Islamic law and European civil law systems. This is often commented upon and now taken for granted in international commercial arbitration. The Chamber system also promoted the procedural predictability I mentioned earlier.

Finally, there was little socialization among the full Tribunal staff. Why do I mention this as a positive factor, in an era when corporate retreats are the norm? Because the political tensions between the Governments would not allow socialization, and it was the wisest course of action not to force it. The exceptions were the lunchroom and the on-and-off table tennis tournament – stories unto themselves. By not pushing for fraternization, most of the staff was able to achieve a high level of daily professional cooperation most of the time.

V. CONCLUSIONS

I started this talk by remembering my initiation with the Tribunal, and my first visit to this building, almost 18 years ago. The 30-some claims I delivered are, I believe, long since concluded. The awards are available in the *Iran-United States Claims Tribunal Reports*, on Westlaw, and some in the *ICCA Yearbook Commercial Arbitration*. The papers themselves remain at Parkweg 13, in the good care of the Registry, to be available to scholars for years to come. This is all solid evidence of the procedural and institutional strength of the Tribunal.

Over these 18 years, I have watched subsequent mass claims systems build upon the Tribunal's strengths to suit their unique missions – copying, adjusting, and rejecting tribunal concepts. It is particularly gratifying to see Tribunal colleagues working with the UNCC, the World Intellectual Property Organization (WIPO), and the Claims Resolution Tribunal for Dormant Swiss Bank Accounts. This is all to the benefit of the claimant communities they serve.

Throughout it all, including this evening, the Permanent Court of Arbitration has provided steady support for the Tribunal and for international dispute resolution. Much of that support goes unpublicized and unapplauded. I know the next speakers will do so as well, but I close with an expression of appreciation to Mr. van den Hout and others.

Institutional and Procedural Aspects of Mass Claims Settlement Systems: The United Nations Compensation Commission

Norbert Wühler *

I. THE MANDATE OF THE UNCC

The UNCC was established in 1991 as a subsidiary organ of the UN Security Council to process claims and pay compensation for losses resulting from Iraq's 1990 invasion and subsequent occupation of Kuwait. Compensation is paid to successful claimants from a special fund that receives a percentage of the proceeds from sales of Iraqi oil. The cease-fire resolution 687 (1991),[1] which was adopted by the Security Council under Chapter VII of the UN Charter, confirmed that Iraq is liable "under international law for any *direct* loss, damage, including environmental damage and the depletion of natural resources, or injury to foreign Governments, nationals and corporations".

While the UNCC is in many respects in the tradition of international claims practice, there are other features that make it a novel and unprecedented system. In particular, it represents the *first* attempt of the international community to organise a claims resolution process through a multinational facility within the UN system. The Commission is *not* a court or an arbitral tribunal before which the parties appear. Rather, it is an administrative body which performs an essentially fact-finding function of examining claims, verifying their validity, evaluating losses and making payment of compensation.

---

* Since 1992, Chief of the Legal Services Branch, United Nations Compensation Commission, Geneva, Switzerland; former Legal Asssistantto the President; former Deputy Secretary-General, Iran-United States Claims Tribunal.

1. The texts of the Security Council resolution 687 adopted on April 3, 1991, and a number of Decisions Taken by the Governing Council of the United Nations Compensation Commission are reproduced as Annex II at pp. 107-116 and pp. 117-165, respectively.

II. THE CLAIMS BEFORE THE UNCC

The institutional and procedural features of the Commission are in large measure determined by the number of claims and the variety of losses brought before it. The UNCC has received over *2.6 million* claims from 96 countries seeking compensation in excess of US$300 billion. In order to facilitate their processing, the claims have been organised into six different categories, according to submitting entity, type of loss and amount claimed. The *vast* majority of the claims came from individuals for relatively small amounts. In contrast to previous claims mechanisms, the individual claims were given priority, both in processing and payment, over the larger claims of individuals and the claims of corporations and Governments. *All* of the smaller individual claims have been processed. Each successful claimant has received at least a partial payment, and it is expected that by the middle of next year *all* small individual claims will have been paid the *full* amount of the compensation awarded which, for these categories, totals approximately US$8.5 billion.

In the meantime, considerable progress has also been made in the processing of the over 10,000 *large* individual claims, the almost 6,000 corporate claims and the 300 claims from Governments and international organisations. The Commission has established a detailed work programme with specific timetables which foresees that the processing of *all remaining* claims will be completed by the end of 2003.

III. INSTITUTIONAL ASPECTS OF THE UNCC

The organisation of the UNCC is characterised by the interplay between *three* organs: a Governing Council, panels of Commissioners and a Secretariat.

The Governing Council, whose membership is the same as that of the UN Security Council at any given time, is the Commission's policy setting body. It has established the criteria for the compensability of claims, the rules of procedure for their processing, the guidelines for the administration of the Compensation Fund and the mechanisms for the payment of compensation. Most importantly, the Governing Council has to approve the compensation awards that Commissioner panels make on the claims. The Council's decisions are final and *not* subject to appeal or review. While the Council may vote and take decisions by majority, it has to date reached *all* of its decisions by consensus.

The evaluation of the claims is performed by panels of Commissioners. They verify the claims, determine whether they are a direct result of Iraq's invasion and occupation of Kuwait, assess the amount of loss or damage and recommend compensation awards to the Governing Council. Commissioner candidates are nominated by the UN Secretary-General and appointed by the Governing Council. Each panel has three members and is established to review a specific category or sub-category of claims. Four panels have already concluded their work, and *fourteen* panels are currently in operation. The Commissioners do not work full time for the Commission. On average, they meet three to four days per month at the seat of the Commission in Geneva and do the remaining work away from Geneva.

The Commission's Secretariat services the Governing Council and the Commissioner panels by providing legal, technical and administrative support. The Secretariat also administers the Compensation Fund and the payment of compensation. The majority of its 240 international staff are lawyers and legal support staff, with the balance made up of accountants, loss adjusters, computer specialists and finance and administrative personnel. Considering that the Commissioners do not work full time on UNCC matters, the Secretariat's role in the preliminary review of the claims and their preparation for review by the panels is substantial.

IV. PROCEDURAL ASPECTS OF THE UNCC

The UNCC procedures are a function of the large number of claims and the size and variety of the losses. The Commissioner panels must apply Security Council resolution 687 (1991) and other relevant Security Council resolutions, the criteria established by the Governing Council for the compensability of losses and in addition, where necessary, other relevant rules of international law. The panels have generally found a sufficient basis in resolution 687 (1991) and the Governing Council decisions for their determinations on the claims and their recommendations of compensation. Occasionally, they have referred to general principles of law, as has the Governing Council itself in some of the criteria for the compensability of business losses.

As is the case in every mass claims programme, a tension exists also in the UNCC between the search for individual justice and fairness and the requirement of an expedient process that resolves all the claims within a reasonable time period. The UNCC's Rules of Procedure do not regulate the proceedings in great detail, but rather leave the Commissioner panels and the Secretariat considerable flexibility to organise the process in the most efficient way. The result has been, as one Commissioner panel put it, that "the vast number of claims [. . .] and the time limits adopted by the Rules, necessitated the employment of legal standards and valuation methods that were administrable and which carefully balanced the twin objectives of speed and accuracy".

For the assessment of the hundreds of thousands of small individual claims, this led to the use of sampling, statistical modelling and computerised matching for the verification and evaluation of the claims. A large database into which all the relevant claims data were entered served as the backbone for many of the operations that were performed in the context of these techniques.

For the larger individual claims and the corporate and Government claims, a *key effort* has been to structure the process in such a way that common legal and valuations issues are determined early on so that the determinations can then be easily applied to subsequent similarly situated claims. To that effect, similar claims have been grouped together and are all submitted to the same panel of Commissioners. There is no adversarial process; rather it is up to the Commissioner panels to establish the facts and evaluate the claims, and to seek the required information and documentation. As such, the process is inquisitorial. The roles of *both* the claimants *and* Iraq are limited, and their participation in the process is determined by the extent to which it is needed by the Commissioner panels to decide the claims. Oral proceedings are the great exception, and *if* they are held it is for the benefit of the Commissioners.

Regarding evidentiary standards, the UNCC has two basic rules. For the expedited small individual claims, "appropriate evidence of the circumstances and amount of the loss" is sufficient, and the evidence need only be the "*reasonable minimum*" that is appropriate under the circumstances. These circumstances include the hasty and difficult conditions in which many of the claimants had to depart from Kuwait or Iraq, often not being able to take their belongings or even their passports and other documents with them. For the larger individual claims and for the corporate and Government claims, a stricter standard requiring "documentary and other appropriate evidence *sufficient to demonstrate* the circumstances and amount of the loss" has been maintained.

For the valuation of the larger claims, the Commission has developed comprehensive and detailed methodologies according to the different loss types, and the Commissioner panels make *considerable* use of outside expert consultants, primarily accountants and loss adjusters, to assist them in these valuations.

A challenge increasingly facing the UNCC, as it would other comparable institutions with numerous decision makers, is how to avoid inconsistencies where similar claims arise out of the same fact patterns and present the same issues but are considered by different panels. With *fourteen* Commissioner panels operating in the UNCC at the same time, and determinations by one panel not being formally binding on other panels, an important technique to ensure consistency has been to group similar claims together and submit them all to the same panel. In a supporting effort, the Secretariat continuously indexes both the determinations of all the panels as well as undetermined issues pending before them, and it makes this information regularly available to all the Commissioners and to the eleven Secretariat teams comprising 70 lawyers who support the panels.

V. CONCLUSION

I would like to conclude with the following. Whether or not the UNCC will be a "success story", will be for others to decide. I submit, however, that it has the potential to *become* one because the following conditions are present:

- continuous political support for the process in the United Nations (through the Governing Council and eventually the Security Council);
- compliance with a work programme with a fixed completion date;
- procedural and operational flexibility;
- innovative techniques relevant to the numbers and types of claims;

- possibility to recruit and maintain dedicated staff with the required experience.

This system has to date resulted in relatively *high* awards for the small individual claims and relatively *low* awards for the larger business claims, the latter often being speculative, not supported by sufficient evidence or altogether outside the Commission's jurisdiction.

These results show that, while the UNCC process accords the claimants and Iraq a much more limited role than that of full parties in a traditional court or arbitration setting, such a process *does* allow for a serious claims review and it *can* produce *overall* fair results notwithstanding that they may be "rough justice" for the particular claimant.

Mass Property Claim Resolution in a Post-War Society: The Commission for Real Property Claims in Bosnia and Herzegovina*

*Hans van Houtte***

I. INTRODUCTION

The restoration of the pre-war property rights of displaced persons and refugees is critical to restore the peace.

This is particularly true for Bosnia and Herzegovina. The devastating impact of the war which ravaged Bosnia from 1992 until 1995 has left a third of the housing stock destroyed or otherwise uninhabitable. The systematic practice of ethnic cleansing forced Bosniacs, Croats and Serbs to seek shelter in areas of Bosnia and Herzegovina where their ethnic group was in the majority or to seek refuge abroad.[1] More than half of the 4,5 million pre-war population of Bosnia and Herzegovina fled their homes in search of safety during the course of the war. According to recent estimates from the UN High Commissioner for Refugees, over 800,000 refugees from Bosnia

* This article is reproduced from (1999) 48 International and Comparative Law Quarterly 625-638 with permission from the publishers The British Institute of International and Comparative Law, 17 Russell Square, London WC1B 5DR.

** Professor of Conflict of Laws, International Business Law and Arbitration, Catholic University of Leuven; Partner, Stibbe Simont Monahan Duhot, Brussels.

The author is member of the Commission for Real Property Claims. All ideas herein express only the personal opinion of the author and do not bind the Commission.

1. By the time the Dayton Peace Agreement was signed in December 1995, more than 1 million Bosnians remained displaced within the borders of Bosnia and Herzegovina. At least 1 million more were living as refugees in some 25 other countries, primarily in the neighbouring republics of former Yugoslavia and throughout Western Europe.

and Herzegovina are still abroad today.[2] Within Bosnia and Herzegovina, more than 800,000 people remain displaced from their pre-conflict homes.[3]

The parties to the Dayton Peace Agreement, which ended the Bosnian war, knew that no lasting peace could be achieved without the resolution of the real property issues of these displaced persons and refugees. Annex 7, Art. I(1) of the General Framework Agreement clearly states the principle:

> "All refugees and displaced persons have the right freely to return to their homes of origin. They shall have the right to have restored to them property of which they were deprived in the course of hostilities since 1991 and to be compensated for any property that cannot be restored to them. The early return of refugees and displaced persons is an important objective of the settlement of the conflict in Bosnia and Herzegovina".[4]

Chapter Two of Annex 7 of the Dayton Peace Agreement created a specific institution, the Commission for Real Property Claims of Displaced Persons and Refugees ("the Commission"), to resolve the sensitive and complicated issues associated with real property. The Commission was mandated to:

> "receive and decide any claims for real property in Bosnia and Herzegovina, where the property has not voluntarily been sold or otherwise transferred since April 1, 1992,[5] and where the claimant does not now enjoy possession of that property. Claims may

2. Outside former Yugoslavia, Germany and Switzerland host the highest numbers. For regular updates of the numbers of Bosnian refugees, see http://www.unhcr.ch/world.
3. Approximately 450,000 displaced persons are in the Federation of Bosnia and Herzegovina and 366,000 in the Republika Srpska. See UNHCR Position on Categories of Persons from Bosnia and Herzegovina who are in Continued Need of International Protection, June 11, 1998.
4. The General Framework Agreement for Peace in Bosnia and Herzegovina, initialled in Dayton on November 21, 1995 and signed in Paris on December 14, 1995 (hereinafter: Dayton Peace Agreement), Annex 7, Art. I, see *infra*, Annex III, pp. 167-192 at pp. 182-188; also reproduced in (1996) 35 International Legal Materials 75 at 138.
5. The day the war started.

be for return of the property or for just compensation in lieu of return."[6]

The Commission, which started its activities in March 1996, may offer interesting features for future mass claims resolution mechanisms in post-war societies.

This paper will concentrate on (A) the main institutional aspects and (B) the methodology of the Commission.[7]

A. Institutional Framework

1. Composition, Structure and Independence of the Commission

The Commission consists of three international members and six national members. The three international commissioners have been appointed by the President of the European Court of Human Rights.[8] The Federation and the Republika Srpska, being the two constituent entities of the Republic of Bosnia and Herzegovina, two Bosniac and two Croat commissioners were appointed by the Federation, while two Serb members were appointed by the Republika Srpska.[9]

6. Dayton Peace Agreement, Annex 7, Art. XI.

7. See for an early analysis of the Commission, H. van Houtte, "The Property Claims Commission in Bosnia and Herzegovina", K. Wellens, ed., *International Law: Theory and Practice. Essays in Honour of Eric Suy* (Martinus Nijhoff, The Hague 1998) pp. 549-563. For a more general discussion, M. Cox, "The Right to Return Home: International Intervention and Ethnic Cleansing in Bosnia and Herzegovina", (1998) 47 International and Comparative Law Quarterly 599. For more extensive and updated information on the Commission, see: http://www.crpc.org.ba.

8. The following international members were appointed for a term of five years: Dr. Jean-Pierre Hocké (chairman), former United Nations High Commissioner for Refugees (Geneva); Prof. Hans van Houtte (legal chair), Catholic University of Leuven (Belgium) and Prof. Maria Rita Saulle, University La Sapienza (Rome).

9. The positions of the respective national members are: Davor Cordas, Vice-Minister for Refugees (Croat); Miroslav Gladanac, former Public Prosecutor (Serb); Jasmin Jahjaefendic, Judge and President of Property Book Court Sarajevo (Bosniac); Damir Ljubic, Federation Deputy Minister for Refugees, Displaced Persons and Social Welfare (Croat); Mirsad Milavic, Secretary-General, Ministry of Refugees, Displaced Persons (Bosniac) and Jovo Miskin, former Director of the Office of Property Registration (Serb).

Under the Dayton Agreements, the Commission can sit in panels.[10] However, a structure of three panels – each consisting of one international and two national members – was clearly not workable since each panel would then miss a representation of the third ethnic group.[11] Consequently the Commission takes its decisions in the plenary meetings.

The Commission's decisions are most often taken by consensus to ensure support for the Commission's work by the three ethnic groups.[12] The deliberations of the Commission are in all events secret and the minutes of the meetings do not reflect individual positions of the various members, in order to avoid any kind of pressure by the respective national authorities.

The Commission has set up an administration of over 250 staff members, based either in the headquarters or in one of the regional claim collection offices throughout Bosnia and Herzegovina[13] or abroad.[14] The Executive Office in Sarajevo is divided into an Operations Department, a Legal Department, an Information Technology Department and a Public Information Department. The vast majority of the staff has been locally recruited. Indeed, the Commission wants to be integrated as much as possible in local society and to provide employment. The Commission has engaged only a few international staff members to oversee the claim collection and claim determination operations.

The settlement of real property rights in a multi-ethnic society, ravaged by war, is obviously a sensitive and risky task. The international commissioners and international staff are granted international protection respectively as diplomatic agents and members of the staff of a mission under the Vienna

10. Annex 7, Art. IX(3).
11. Instead, two working groups have been established: one concentrates on legal questions, the other deals with operational issues.
12. However, decisions can be taken by simple majority. Where there is no majority, the chairman's vote is decisive. For substantial matters the majority should also include the votes of two international members. General regulations, regulations of proceedings and criteria for the settlement of individual claims, by-laws of the Commission, administration and organisation of work, criteria for valuation of properties, are considered substantial matters.
13. I.e., Banja Luka, Brcko, Lukavica, Mostar, Sarajevo and Tuzla. Moreover, offices in Bihac and Vitez are planned.
14. I.e., in Croatia, present Yugoslavia, Montenegro, Denmark, Germany, The Netherlands, Norway and Sweden.

Convention on Diplomatic Relations (1961).[15] However, the national commissioners and the local staff who remain most exposed to possible criticism of the local community, were not granted specific immunities or protection by the Dayton Agreement. The Commission therefore has included in the Headquarters Agreement which it has concluded with the Republic of Bosnia and Herzegovina that the Republic has in a more general way "to take all necessary measures to ensure the protection, safety and security of the Commission and its members and staff in the performance of their duties and to ensure the security of its premises and facilities".[16] The Headquarters Agreement moreover specifically recognises that the national commissioners and staff enjoy the immunities provided under the Vienna Convention to the extent necessary for them to fulfil their mandate. It also explicitly states that they "shall not be held criminally or civilly liable for any acts carried out in furtherance of their responsibilities".[17]

2. The Commission Is a Public International Institution

The operation of a commission mandated to restore property rights in a post-war situation should obviously not depend on the domestic law of the country where the property is located.[18] Legislative and political developments should not jeopardise the independence and efficiency of such body. Consequently, the Commission is not subject to domestic Bosnia and Herzegovina law but to international law.

The international personality of the Commission follows from the fact that it was established in Annex 7 of the Dayton Agreements. It has been accepted that Annex 7, signed by the Republic as well as by the Federation

15. The privileges and immunities granted to international commissioners and their families under Annex 7, Art. VIII(3), were extended to international staff and their families under the Headquarters Agreement of September 4, 1996, Art. 1, para. 3.
16. Headquarters Agreement, Art. 1, para. 3.
17. *Idem.*, Art. 2, para. 2.
18. This is even more so in the specific case of the federal State of Bosnia and Herzegovina, where property matters are within the competence of the constituent entities and not of the federal authorities.

and the Republika Srpska, constitutes an international treaty.[19] Moreover, Annex 7 is attached to the General Framework Agreement, in which the Republics of Croatia and Yugoslavia "welcomed and endorsed the arrangements that have been made" and committed themselves to "fully respect and promote fulfillment of the commitments made therein".[20] Furthermore, the European Union Special Negotiator as well as France, Germany, Russia, the United Kingdom and the United States signed the General Framework Agreement as witnesses. As an attachment to the General Framework Agreement, Annex 7 is part of this treaty and is thus also governed by international law. According to well-established principles and in the absence of counter-indications, the Commission – created by a text of international law – thus constitutes a body governed by international law.[21]

The international character of the Commission has been formally recognised by the Republic of Bosnia and Herzegovina by concluding a Headquarters Agreement with the Commission. This agreement explicitly confirms that it is "an *international* independent body" and that it possesses "legal personality".[22] By recognising the international character of the Commission, the Republic has waived any pretence to "domesticate" it.

The Commission is an independent international body.[23] In fact, it is an international body of a specific kind. It is namely a "public international

---

19. Although the Federation and the Republika Srpska became mere "composing entities" of the Republic, they nevertheless possessed an international personality when the Dayton Agreements were signed. See e.g. P. Gaeta, "The Dayton Agreements and International Law", (1996) 7 European Journal of International Law 147 at 158-160.
20. Dayton Peace Agreement, Art. VI.
21. See, e.g., H. Schermers, *International Institutional Law* (Martinus Nijhoff, The Hague 1995) § 45.
22. Headquarters Agreement of September 4, 1996, Art. 1, para. 1. This Agreement was signed only by the Republic of Bosnia and Herzegovina and not by the entities. However, under the Dayton Agreements and also under the Constitution, both entities are bound by agreements concluded by the Republic. It was unnecessary and politically unacceptable to list the entities as parties to the Agreement.
23. In the early phases of its operations, the Commission has deemed it useful to rely on the institutional infrastructure of the International Organization for Migration (IOM) for help in the administration of its finances. The Commission, being a small operation with limited manpower, preferred to focus on its specific tasks while financial and budgetary matters were passed to the IOM. Since January 1998, the Commission itself has taken over that responsibility.

institution" (in French "*un établissement public international*").[24] A public international institution is created by international treaty, which grants such an institution a foundation in international law. However, it distinguishes itself from an international organisation *stricto sensu* as it renders services to private parties and takes care of the needs of citizens while international organisations *stricto sensu* focus, rather, on the interests of States. A public international institution has its own specific competences, its own budget and financial sources.[25] The Commission is a *public* institution as it carries out a public service, i.e. the settlement of property claims, which in normal conditions would be done by a domestic public institution. Moreover, it is an *international* institution, as it is created by a treaty, "denationalised", autonomous and free from national political interests and control.

Some may argue that, in principle, international public institutions have to render services to parties from more than one country while the Commission's mandate is limited to claims for real property located in one single State Bosnia and Herzegovina. Despite that limitation, the international scope of the Commission's work cannot be questioned. Clearly, the Commission renders services to other States and individuals located outside Bosnia by settling property claims of Bosnian refugees and thus facilitating their return to Bosnia and Herzegovina. Several Western European countries which host Bosnian refugees have, for instance, requested the Commission to collect claims from Bosnian refugees within their territory. In addition, the Commission's operations are financed by several States.[26]

The international status of the Commission may, however, be limited in time. Indeed, Art. IX of Annex 7 states that after the first five years all commissioners have to be appointed by the presidency of the Republic. Art. XVI adds that after five years the responsibility for the financing and operation of the Commission will be transferred to the Bosnia and

---

24. See H.T. Adam, *Les organismes internationaux spécialisés, Contribution à la théorie générale des établissements publics internationaux* (LGDJ, Paris 1992). The ECJ has, e.g., recognised the "European Laying-up Fund for Inland Waterway Vessels" as a public international institution (*Opinion 1/76* of 26 April 1977, [1977] European Court Reports 741, 755 et seq.).
25. Adam, *idem.*, p. 3.
26. Contributions are made by the EU, the US and among others Italy, The Netherlands, Canada, Switzerland, Sweden, Germany, Norway, Belgium, Austria, Ireland and Luxembourg.

Herzegovina Government, unless agreed otherwise.[27] Consequently, when the appointment of its members and its financing have come exclusively into the hands of the Republic of Bosnia and Herzegovina, the Commission will become a merely national public institution.

3. Relations with Other International Bodies

The Commission, though fully independent, forms part of a cluster of international bodies, created by the Dayton Agreement: "The Commission shall cooperate with other entities established under the General Framework Agreement, agreed by the Parties, or authorised by the United Nations Security Council".[28] The modalities of this co-operation, however, needed to be worked out.

For instance, the Commission needed to establish its relationship with the "High Representative" who is entrusted by the "Community of States" with monitoring and co-ordinating the civilian implementation of the Dayton Agreements and the Security Council resolution.[29] At present, the Commission has frequent contacts and working sessions with the Office of the High Representative, which considers the Commission to be one of the key players in the peace process.

The Commission also had to define its relationship with the Commission on Human Rights, i.e. the Office of the Human Rights Ombudsman and the Chamber on Human Rights, created under Annex 6 to the Dayton Agreement to secure the respect of human rights in Bosnia and Herzegovina.[30] Indeed, the property rights, which have to be settled by the Commission, are at the same time protected as a human right, and thus fall under the jurisdiction of Annex 6 institutions.[31] Both the Commission and the Commission on

---

27. At this stage, it is unclear whether the other States will continue to finance the Commission after the initial five-years period.
28. Annex 7, Art. X(5).
29. Annex 10, reproduced in Annex III at pp. 189-192, and S.C. Res. 1031 of December 15, 1995.
30. See *infra*, Annex III, pp. 172-181.
31. As claimants are able to submit a claim regarding the property issue before both the Commission and the Human Rights Chamber, those two bodies should avoid rendering a decision in the same case. The Dayton Agreements state that the Chamber should not address any claim which is substantially the same as a matter

Human Rights seem thus to have concurring competencies with regard to property rights.[32] In fact, many of the cases submitted to the Commission on Human Rights actually concern real estate issues. However, proceedings before the Commission on Human Rights and the Commission are completely different in scope and in outcome: before the latter, the claimant requests the recognition of his property right in view of the return to or disposition of his property; before the Commission on Human Rights the claimant seeks redress from the domestic authorities because of their violation of his human right to property. In this way proceedings before the Commission may somehow chronologically precede proceedings before the Commission on Human Rights: it is for the former to determine property rights, for the latter to intervene when the authorities fail to implement this property right and facilitate return.

The Commission, finally, had to clarify its relationship and seek ways of co-operation with the UN High Commissioner for Refugees (UNHCR), the leading agency involved in the return of refugees and displaced persons and thus inevitably also concerned about property rights.[33]

---

which has already been the subject of another settlement procedure (Annex 6, Art. VIII). A permanent exchange of information about cases, which have been submitted respectively to the Commission and the office of the Ombudsman or Commission on Human Rights, is therefore necessary. The possibility has been considered that the Commission on Human Rights could request the Commission to issue opinions on property matters subject of proceedings before the Commission on Human Rights. However, no specific mechanism for such a "preliminary ruling" has so far been elaborated.

32. It has been suggested that there could be a right of appeal against Commission decisions before the Annex 6 institutions. This possibility of judicial review seems to be contrary to the principle that Commission decisions are final (Annex 7, Art. XII(7)).
33. Initially, the risk of confusion with the UNHCR was substantial as in the Dayton Agreements the Commission was called merely the "Commission for Displaced Persons and Refugees". In order to make it clear that the Commission did not aim to be active on refugee problems in general, already during its first session it changed its name to the "Commission for Real Property Claims of Displaced Persons and Refugees".

B. Operation Framework

The Commission's basic mandate is formulated in Art. XI of Annex 7 of the Dayton Peace Agreement:

> "The Commission shall receive and decide any claims for real property in Bosnia and Herzegovina, where the property has not voluntarily been sold or otherwise transferred since April 1, 1992, and where the claimant does not now enjoy possession of that property".

One of the Commission's earliest tasks was to translate that mandate into concrete rules and regulations. It thus started its activities with, *inter alia*, drafting a book of regulations, in which the claim registration procedure and the substantive standards for claim determination are laid down. The essential features of claim registration and determination will be discussed later.

1. Nature of Real Property Claims

a. Claim Collection Office

Persons displaced within Bosnia and Herzegovina who have lost their property in the course of the conflict can lodge a claim in one of the Commission's regional offices within Bosnia and Herzegovina. The Commission started with regional offices in Sarajevo, Mostar and Lukavica, i.e. in each of the areas within Bosnia and Herzegovina respectively controlled by Bosniacs, Croats and Serbs. In 1997 three offices in Brcko were added. In 1998 new offices were opened in Banja Luka and Tuzla. More offices are planned in Bihac and Vitez. Moreover, mobile claim-collection teams cover remote areas within Bosnia and Herzegovina.

Many, who took refuge outside Bosnia and Herzegovina, can file a claim in the country where they are staying. Indeed, countries with a substantial number of Bosnia and Herzegovina refugees support the opening of a claim-collection office to facilitate the return of these refugees. In 1997 three offices were thus opened in Montenegro. In 1998 claims-collection offices were opened in Germany (Berlin), Norway, present Yugoslavia, Sweden and Denmark. In 1999 more claims-collection offices will be opened in, among other places, Croatia, Austria, The Netherlands and Germany.

b. Claim Registration Proceedings

Claims-collection involves two stages. In the first stage the prospective claimant is interviewed by a Commission staff member who checks whether a claim falls within the Commission's mandate. The claimant is informed both orally and in writing about the claim registration procedure. Information is given on issues such as what outcomes the claimant can expect from the Commission, which documents should be presented to support a claim, etc. If the claim cannot be processed immediately, the claimant also receives an appointment for the formal claim registration at a specific date and time.

At the actual claims-collection, a Commission staff member interviews the claimant individually and screens the documentary evidence presented. In the particular post-war context in which the Commission is operating, up to one third of claimants are not in a position to submit adequate documents proving their property rights. In these cases, the claimant needs to give all possible information about the claimed property.

All relevant information is immediately entered into a claims computer database. A claim form is then printed in duplicate and shown to the claimant, who is asked to review it for accuracy and to sign it for approval. The Commission retains a signed copy of the claim as well as a copy of the presented evidence. By the end of February 1999, a total of over 126,000 claims relating to almost 160,000 properties were registered in this manner.[34] It is expected that overall up to 500,000 claims may be submitted.

To process this vast number of claims in the most expedient and efficient manner possible, the Commission had necessarily to limit the scope of the proceedings. It does not hear claimants but renders decisions only on the basis of the claim document and the available evidence. Consequently, accurate claim registration, which has to allow efficient processing by computer, is crucial. A comprehensive, detailed and user-friendly claim form, which contains all information relevant for the efficient computer processing of the claims, has been developed. The claim form includes three main sections: (i) details about the claimants and registered right holders, (ii)

34. 53% of all claimed properties are located in the Federation territory; 47% in the Republika Srpska.

details about the claimed real property and (iii) details about the scope of property rights and the evidence presented to prove such rights.

c. *Scope of the Claims*

i. Recognition of Ownership or Possession

The Commission merely recognises the ownership or property right and leaves it to the claimant to select the remedy of his choice once his ownership/property right has been recognised. On the basis of such recognition, the possessor can exercise his right to possession; the owner can either offer the property for rent, return to it or dispose of it at a later stage.

However, the claimants may indicate their personal preference for one of three basic options: (i) return into possession, (ii) compensation for lost property or (iii) mere confirmation of property rights. These options are in no way binding upon the claimant. Moreover they have no bearing on the Commission's decision. However, they provide useful and interesting statistical information about the preferences of displaced persons and refugees and indirectly about the property situation in the country.

Under the first option, the claimant can express his or her intention to return into possession of the real property in question. This option, which was considered the gateway to the restoration of a multi-ethnic society in the Dayton negotiations, has been chosen by 54% of all claimants.[35]

The second option envisages compensation. However, compensation is rather difficult to realise. It is a delicate matter to determine the value of the property at the outbreak of hostilities, i.e. in April 1992.[36] Moreover, it would be impossible to organise specific evaluations for each property. On the other hand, fair fixed rates for compensation on the basis of surface area, number of rooms and available infrastructure are not easy to determine. Claimants are told very clearly that no money is available for compensation

35. It is politically relevant that approximately 80% of the Bosniac claims, 50% of the Croat claims and 10% of the Serb claims concern the option to return.
36. See Annex 7, Art. XII(4).

at present.[37] The Dayton Peace Agreements have indicated that compensation should not necessarily consist of payment of a sum of money but could also consist of a compensation bond for the future purchase of real estate.[38] These bonds could also be used to facilitate or promote the voluntary exchange of property. However, bond schemes cannot yet be set up and are unlikely to be organised in the near future. Nevertheless 24% of all claimants still have opted for compensation.

Under the third option the claimant merely requests the Commission to confirm his or her ownership or lawful possession of the property. It thus allows a claimant who has not yet decided what to do with the property to keep all options open. At present, approximately 20% of the claimants have chosen option three.

ii. Setting Aside Contract

Many of those who fled or were imprisoned were forced – at gunpoint or through systematic harassment – to sign contracts and transfer their property. The claimant may ask the Commission to set aside a wartime sale or transfer concluded under duress. The Dayton Agreements explicitly empower the Commission to declare such contracts null and void: "any illegal property transaction, including any transfer that was made under duress, in exchange for exit permission or documents, or that was otherwise in connection with ethnic cleansing" is invalid.[39]

In fact the Commission does not require proof of "ethnic cleansing" or a proven causality between a specific "act of ethnic cleansing" and a transfer of property. In principle, any wartime sale or transfer is presumed to have

37. Option two raises, moreover, a more fundamental issue. Indeed, the possibility of receiving compensation might induce refugees not to return to their places of origin but to remain abroad or to stay in a territory controlled by their ethnic group. Thus compensation could negatively affect the return of refugees and restoration of a multi-ethnic society. In Art. I(1) of Annex 7, compensation was envisaged only when the owner could not return to his or her property. However, it was felt that the full respect of property rights entails the free choice between return or compensation. Therefore, under Art. XII(5) the owner had the right to seek compensation "in lieu of return".
38. Art. XII(6).
39. Annex 7, Art. XII(3).

been made under circumstances that justify setting aside the transaction at the request of one of the parties. Of course this may be complicated by the fact that the property has since been transferred to a third party. Once the contract is cancelled and what has been exchanged has been restored, the former owner may exercise one of the three basic options, mentioned above. At present, only a very small number of claimants has requested a wartime transfer of property to be set aside.

iii. Return to Abandoned Houses and Apartments

In Bosnia and Herzegovina houses are privately owned. The majority of apartments, however, were socially owned. They belonged to companies, government organs or social organisations which gave their employees a so-called "occupancy right" (*stanarsko pravo*).[40] This occupancy right is a complex quasi-ownership right, stronger than a tenancy right but less than full ownership. A right for life, it can be inherited by family members but cannot be sold. Occupancy right holders not only paid rent for their apartments, but had also to contribute to the Housing Contribution Fund. Before the war, the Government started privatising socially owned apartments so that occupancy right holders could convert their occupancy right into full ownership .

During the war, many apartments had to be vacated. Within the Federation and the Republika Srpska statutes declared that an occupancy right holder temporarily lost his right to use the apartment if he left the premises after April 30, 1991. The municipal authorities could then allocate the abandoned apartment to others. Similar statutes existed for abandoned houses. At the end of the war an occupant of an abandoned apartment or house had to return and commence using the premises within seven days (if displaced within the country) or within 15 days (in case of refugees abroad) after the proclamation of the cessation of the state of war. If the pre-war occupant did not return within these deadlines, the apartment or house was considered permanently abandoned and the pre-war occupant irrevocably lost his or her occupancy right. In fact, most people could not have returned within such a short period of time to their apartment or house, which, moreover, was often still

40. Occupancy rights were subject to substantial regulation before the war, in particular under the Law on Housing Relations.

occupied by the new user.[41] The Commission disregards such legislation, which violates human rights, i.e. the right to property.

Under pressure from the international community, new statutes have set aside the wartime laws on abandoned property and apartments. These statutes allow a pre-war occupant to claim repossession of an apartment or a house with the municipal housing authority at the place where the apartment or house is located. The municipal authorities must decide within 30 days. These decisions should confirm the pre-war occupancy rights, terminate the rights of current users, and set a deadline by which the current user of the apartment must move out. For private property such as houses, if the property is vacant or occupied illegally, the owner may move in immediately following the decision. If the private property is occupied by an authorised temporary user, the current occupant has in principle 90 days to vacate the property.[42]

However, when the pre-war occupant of an apartment or owner of a house is not satisfied with the domestic proceedings or decisions, he may also file a claim for return with the Commission:

> "A party affected by a decision [made by the municipality] may at any time file a claim with the Property Commission. In the event that such a claim is filed, all proceedings including execution of decisions or order shall be stayed pending the final decision of the Property Commission. A decision of the Property Commission is final and binding".[43]

---

41. The unrealistic nature of the deadline can be illustrated by the numbers for Sarajevo: of the 13,500 occupancy right holders who left Sarajevo, less than 200 returned within the deadline.
42. See for the Federation: the Law on the Cessation of the Application of the Law on Temporarily Abandoned Real Property Owned by Citizens and the Law on the Cessation of the Application of the Law on Abandoned Apartments, *Official Gazette* of the Federation of Bosnia and Herzegovina 11/98, April 3, 1998. See for the Republika Srpska: the Law on the Cessation of Application of the Law on the Use of Abandoned Property, voted by the National Assembly of Republika Srpska on December 2, 1998.
43. E.g., Art. 14 of both the Law on the Cessation of the Application of the Law on Temporarily Abandoned Real Property Owned by Citizens and the Law on the Cessation of the Application of the Law on Abandoned Apartments.

For displaced persons and refugees who are unable to obtain relief through the domestic authorities, the Commission thus serves as a back-up mechanism or appeal tribunal.

The implementation of a decision which grants return to an apartment is, however, at present greatly hindered by provisions in the respective statutes of both entities which allow the authorities to allocate "another apartment" to a pre-war occupancy right holder.[44] As no satisfactory objective criteria have been formulated by the entities to justify the refusal to return to one's own apartment, the High Representative suspended these provisions in November 1998. The entities' reaction hitherto (March 1999) has been to refuse to implement the decisions at all and effectively prevent a substantial number of Commission certificate holders from returning to possession of their pre-war apartments.

iv. *Prima Facie* Verification for Reconstruction Purposes

Many houses have been destroyed and need to be reconstructed. International reconstruction agencies and non-governmental organisations, however, prefer to be certain that they are reconstructing a dwelling for the rightful occupant. At their request the Commission delivers so-called "*prima facie* notifications" or "indications of property rights" on specific dwellings and checks the legal status of the beneficiaries of the reconstruction aid.[45]

The Commission also provided more than 8,000 *prima facie* notifications to the Office of the High Representative for Brcko, Ambassador Farrand, to assist in the return of displaced persons and refugees to the area.

44. Federation Law on the Cessation of Application of the Law on Abandoned Apartments, Art. 3(6); Republika Srpska Law on the Cessation of Application of the Law on the Use of Abandoned Property, Art. 17.

45. These notifications do not constitute final Commission decisions; they are mere checks against the pre-war cadastre records and the 1991 census.

2. Claim Determination

a. Evidence

Evidence collection, verification and decision-making on property claims in post-war Bosnia and Herzegovina are extremely difficult. Traditionally, property records were kept in two forms:

(1) land cadastres, held by the Geodetic Administration and containing information about the properties themselves, and (2) property books, kept by the courts, in which the rights to real properties, including mortgages and other burdens, were recorded. Moreover, a third of all property books were destroyed before or during the war and many other records were taken away or tampered with. Furthermore, a new cadastre, which would merge the land cadastre and the property books, was in preparation in several municipalities since 1984, but finalised only in a few places.

The Commission is in possession of the pre-war cadastre databases for approximately half the 109 municipalities. For the other municipalities and for all cases where the cadastre database does not provide a conclusive determination, verification officers are sent to the property book courts and the administrative bodies to check the claim against all available property records.[46] Where no records are available or accessible, the lawyers need to examine documents from different authorities, including verified contracts, court decisions, decrees of administrative authorities, etc. The process of claim-determination is extremely intensive. It involves scrutiny of evidence from a number of different sources. Moreover, whenever documentary evidence is conflicting, it is extremely difficult to reconcile the data obtained.

b. Decision

The Commission bases its decisions concerning real property located in Bosnia on the former Yugoslav property law, which was applicable in Bosnia as "*lex rei sitae*" on the eve of the war. Moreover, it takes into account wartime and post-wartime statutory provisions of the entities to the extent

46. Art. XII(1) of Annex 7 specifies that the Commission shall be entitled to have access to any and all property records in Bosnia and Herzegovina and to any and all real property located in Bosnia and Herzegovina for purposes of inspection, evaluation and assessment related to the consideration of a claim.

that these provisions respect human rights. Indeed, the Commission can apply or consider only domestic law which is consistent with Annex 7. It has thus decided that it will not apply the entities' statutes which limit the right of claimants to return to their apartments (see *supra*).

Furthermore, the Commission applies former Yugoslav conflict of law principles to find the legal system applicable to preliminary issues such as inheritance, marriage etc., which sometimes have to be resolved in deciding on property rights.

Decision-making is centralised in the headquarters in Sarajevo. Decision proposals are prepared by a multi-ethnic team of more than 45 lawyers and entered into the decision software. This advanced software was specifically designed to incorporate all the possible legal variations in decision-making and to ensure the most efficient and expedient processing of all claims. Four commissioners, composing the Legal Working Group, then review the decision proposals and present them for adoption to the plenary session.

Once the Commission at its monthly plenary session has adopted the final decisions, official certificates are printed and delivered to the claimants.

Under the Dayton Peace Agreement, the Commission's decisions are final.[47] However, in the absence of accurate and reliable property records, the Commission has deemed it wise to allow an exceptional right of reconsideration to claimants and interested third parties. Indeed, it may reconsider its decision if the claimant or any other person with a legal interest in the designated real property, within 60 days of learning of the decision or of obtaining new evidence which could materially affect the decision, presents such evidence to the Commission.

By February 1999 the Commission had adopted more than 31,000 decisions, with at present a monthly rate of over 4,000 decisions. Only a few requests for reconsideration have as yet been lodged.

The Commission could not render decisions immediately after it was created. During the initial phases of its operations, it had to lay the groundwork for its claim-collection and claim-determination processes. Moreover,

---

47. Annex 7, Art. XII(7).

a lack of funds delayed the start-up of operations and still prevents the Commission from achieving its full potential. The pace of decision-making has, however, increased dramatically in recent months and will continue to increase as standards for decision-making are further elaborated.

According to the Dayton Agreements, a Commission certificate confirms the pre-war rights of the claimant and entitles him or her to resume possession of the designated property or to transfer (sell, exchange or lease) the property. Where appropriate, the decisions form a sufficient legal basis for the property records to be changed. The certificate also contains a clause to the effect that:

> "All legal acts passed by competent Republic of Bosnia-Herzegovina or Entity administrative or judicial bodies after April 1, 1992, i.e. the outbreak of war, which cancelled or restricted the legal rights to the designated real property of the claimants and all legal transactions concluded after April 1992 without the free will of those persons, which gave rise to a change in the legal or factual status of the designated real property, are made ineffective by this decision".

The implementation of the Commission's decisions by the local authorities remains, however, the critical issue. Under the Dayton Peace Agreement the federal republic and the constituent entities of Bosnia and Herzegovina are explicitly and specifically responsible for the enforcement of Commission decisions. Indeed, Annex 7 provides that the Federation, the Republika Srpska and the Federal Republic of Bosnia and Herzegovina must "respect and implement decisions expeditiously and in good faith".

At present local bodies are, however, still rather reluctant to carry out the international obligation undertaken by their central authority. The Court of Sarajevo, for instance, has gone into great detail to explain that implementation was not a matter for the court but for the administration – a view which is not correct but nevertheless effectively delays implementation. Continuous and steady increases in the number of rendered decisions will add to the existing pressure on the competent local authorities to fulfil their strict obligation to implement Commission decisions. The more certificates issued the more property rights confirmed by the Commission will be recognised.

II. CONCLUSION

The Commission offers an original and efficient formula for settling real property claims in post-war societies. The decisions rendered by this impartial, independent and international body will in the long term serve as a formal recognition of property title and thus enhance legal security. They provide the legal basis for return to or renting, exchange or sale of real estate. Indeed, the Commission is the only body which can efficiently provide such formal recognition of property title.

It would be unrealistic to expect that the Commission's decisions, which go against the political and even financial interests of the local power structure, will immediately be fully recognised or implemented by the local authorities. However, even if implementation in the short term may give rise to some problems, the decisions have been formally taken and are in the hands of the public. Sooner or later they have to be implemented. In Germany owners had to wait for 50 years but their titles to property located in the former German Democratic Republic were finally recognised after the reunification. It is to be hoped that justice will be done more quickly in Bosnia and Herzegovina.

Institutional and Procedural Aspects of Mass Claims Litigation and Settlement: The *Exxon Valdez* and *Bhopal Gas Disaster* Cases

Kenneth F. McCallion *

I. INTRODUCTION

Major disasters have a tendency to produce derivative disasters in the litigation, settlement and claims processes that follow. Great care must be given to the design, organization and administration of the judicial or dispute resolution mechanism that is selected so that the "cure" does not end up compounding the wrong. The *Exxon Valdez* and *Bhopal* litigations are contrasting case studies of how two major disasters, having significant similarities, can result in very different procedural histories and results.

II. THE *EXXON VALDEZ* CASE

In the early morning hours of March 24, 1989, the "Exxon Valdez", owned by the Exxon Shipping Corporation, ran aground near Bligh Reef in Prince William Sound, Alaska, spilling approximately eleven million gallons of crude oil owned by the Exxon Corporation. Captain Joseph Hazelwood, the master of the vessel and a known alcoholic, boarded the vessel after having spent a day of heavy drinking in Valdez, Alaska, with other crew members. The evidence indicated that he had consumed at least eight vodka doubles, and his blood alcohol level was more than six times the permissible level under Coast Guard regulations. Hazelwood took the "Exxon Valdez" outside established shipping lanes in order to avoid ice, but, inexplicably, he

* Litigation Attorney, specializing in environmental and human rights cases; Partner, Goodkind Labaton Rudoff & Sucharow LLP, New York; previously served as Assistant United States Attorney, a Special Attorney for the US Department of Justice, and Deputy First Assistant Attorney General for New York State. Mr. McCallion represents various native Alaskan corporations in the *Exxon Valdez* litigation and, in the *Bhopal Gas Disaster* litigation cases, he represents the victims and their organizations in a class action case pending in federal court in New York.

put the vessel on automatic pilot, causing it to accelerate directly towards Bligh Reef. Hazelwood then left the bridge in violation of federal pilotage regulations, leaving vague instructions to an inexperienced and fatigued junior officer, Gregory Cousins.

The result of Exxon's reckless conduct and gross mismanagement was the largest oil spill and greatest environmental disaster in American history. Over the next several days, ocean currents and winds pushed the spilled oil in a southwesterly direction onto the shores of lands owned by several Alaska native corporations, comprising more than one million acres of wilderness land along the western Prince William Sound, about the size of Rhode Island. Native Alaskans, who subsist through fishing, gathering and harvesting, not only saw their salmon and herring resources decimated, but found their ability to hunt and gather shellfish, marine mammals, and plants affected as well.

Within weeks, the crude oil that had not washed up on the Sound's beaches was churned into a thick mousse, which washed up on the shores of lands outside the Sound, more than 600 miles from Bligh Reef. These wilderness properties were located on the southern Kenai Peninsula, the Kodiak Archipelago and the Alaska Peninsula.[1] The commercial fishing economy of the south-central Alaskan coastal communities was devastated, affecting nearly everyone in the area, including commercial and sports fishermen, fish processors and their employees, and related businesses such as tenderers, expediters, and fishing and processing equipment providers. The first fishing seasons, due to open in April, were cancelled, and within two months, the Alaska Department of Fish and Game closed or substantially curtailed almost all fisheries in the affected area. The oil spill affected over 60,000 people and resulted in both short and long term environmental damage, the full extent of which was virtually impossible to fully qualify. The spilled oil impaired the spawning of returning fish, the ability of juvenile fish to leave their stream birthplaces, and the spawning of returning fish in critical feed grounds along the shorelines. Experts retained to try to quantify the damages included shoreline ecologists, geologists, biologists, economists, and archeologists. The hard data collected was used to develop predictive

1. No lawsuits, to our knowledge, were brought for damage caused to the global commons. These damages would include the atmospheric pollution caused by the evaporating oil, and the contamination of the ocean caused by spilled oil that never reached land.

models estimating the period of time needed for each affected shoreline segment to return to something approaching its unpolluted pre-spill condition.

1. The Federal Trial

Following the grounding of the "Exxon Valdez", dozens of class action and individual direct lawsuits were filed in Alaska state and federal court on behalf of more than 60,000 individuals, businesses, native corporations and local governments, seeking both compensatory and punitive damages. The federal cases were consolidated in the Alaska District Court in Anchorage before Judge Russel Holland, who entered a stipulated order certifying three classes: A Commercial Fishing Class, a Native Class, and a Landowner Class. Plaintiffs' counsel were organized under the direction of a court-approved Plaintiffs Coordinating Committee (PCC), which managed a common litigation fund, coordinated the discovery process and, ultimately, conducted the trials on behalf of the plaintiffs. While Judge Brian Shortell of the Alaska State Superior Court ruled that normal proximate cause standards and a state strict liability statute would determine whether plaintiffs with cases filed in state court could recover their losses, the federal district court held that under *Robins Dry Dock and Repair Co. v. Flint*, 275 U.S. 303 (1927), only commercial and subsistence fisherman and those suffering direct physical impact from Exxon's oil could recover. This led the defendants to remove most of the state court actions to federal court, where they obtained summary judgments dismissing approximately 40,000 economic damage claims under *Robins Dry Dock.* The cases filed by the native Alaskan corporations and certain municipal landowners were among those removed by Exxon to federal court, but motions to remand these cases to state court were ultimately granted by Judge Holland. Consequently, the only plaintiffs who had their compensatory damage cases tried in state court were five native Alaskan corporations and a few municipal corporations. The remainder of the compensatory damage cases were tried in federal court.

In addition to removing most of the cases to federal court, Exxon also requested that the federal court certify a mandatory punitive damage class, consisting of all persons (including those with cases remaining in state court) seeking punitive damages. The federal judge granted this motion, resulting in the trial one unified punitive damage discovery and trial in federal court.

The federal district judge carefully managed this complex litigation, entering literally hundreds of orders. In addition, a special discovery master entered hundreds of additional orders. With court supervision and approval, the parties agreed to a Trial Plan providing for four separate phases of the trial. The first three phases would be tried to a single jury of 12 (rather than the customary six), with a unanimous verdict required.

Phase I began on May 9, 1994, five years after the spill, and lasted approximately one month. Since Exxon stipulated that its negligence had caused the disaster, the sole issue was whether Exxon and Captain Hazelwood had acted recklessly and in gross disregard of a known duty. Such a finding was a necessary and critical element of any punitive damage award. The jury returned a verdict that both Exxon and Hazelwood were reckless. The evidence presented at trial tended to establish that the finding of recklessness on the part of Exxon was based both on the grossly negligent conduct of its upper management in failing to establish and enforce safety procedures, including the monitoring, treatment and supervision of Captain Hazelwood, as well as Exxon's vicarious liability for the reckless conduct of Hazelwood himself.

Phase IIA went to trial in federal court in Anchorage on June 20, 1994, to determine certain compensatory damage issues, such as the lost fishing harvests, lost price and fishing permit valuation claims. The Phase IIA Special Verdict Form contained 26 special interrogatories, some with as many as ten subparts. The jury deliberated for one full month (from July 11, 1994 to August 11, 1994), and awarded $287 million in compensatory damages based on these claims.

Phase IIB of the federal trial, which was to determine the claims of the Alaska Native Class based upon the commodity value of the lost substance fishing harvests, was settled for $22.6 million.

Phase III, where the jury was asked to decide whether Exxon and/or Hazelwood's reckless conduct should result in an assessment of punitive damages, resulted, on September 16, 1994, in a $5 billion verdict against Exxon, and against Hazelwood in the amount of $5,000.

Phase IV, which was to determine the amount of compensatory damages of plaintiffs whose damages were not determined in Phase II – including landowners and participants in various commercial fisheries – was settled before trial in mid-1996.

Exxon and Hazelwood filed over two-dozen post-trial motions, resulting in approximately 250 pages of rulings by the federal district court judge. Final judgment was entered on September 24, 1996, with an amended judgment entered on January 30, 1997. In short, despite Exxon's protestations to the contrary, of virtually all objective observers found that the federal court trials were conducted in an eminently fair and diligent matter, with the defendants having the benefit of numerous procedural advantages, including favorable instructions and evidentiary rulings, as well as exhaustive post-trial review.

Exxon's appeal of the $5 billion punitive damage verdict is presently *sub judice* before a Ninth Circuit Court of Appeals panel in Seattle, having been fully briefed and argued. In essence, Exxon is claiming immunity from punitive damages based upon its settlement with the federal government and State of Alaska for over $1 billion dollars. Exxon's argument is that punitive damages is, by its very nature, vindication of a harm to the public in general, and that the settlement with the governments should have precluded any trial by the private plaintiffs. In the pending appeal, the plaintiffs are arguing that the fact that Exxon agreed to make limited payments for public harm in its settlements with the United States and Alaska creates no bar to traditional punitive damages in tort litigation by persons who suffered private harm as a foreseeable result of Exxon's reckless and reprehensible conduct. Plaintiffs point out that punitive damages have long been recognized in common law jurisdiction to punish reckless tortfeasors and to help ensure that the wrongful conduct will not be repeated. The plaintiffs' position on appeal is supported by a 1991 consent decree entered into by the federal and state governments in a case brought before Judge Stanley Sporkin of the federal district court in Washington, D.C. Certain native Alaskan corporations had intervened in the federal court action brought in Washington, D.C. by the state and federal governments against Exxon for spill-related claims. The native corporations sought injunctive relief to protect their own state court claims from being impaired. In September 1991, the federal and state governments entered into a revised consent decree recognizing that the native corporations retained all private claims for private harms resulting from the oil spills, including natural resource damage claims arising from damage to the native corporations' private landholdings.

2. The TAPL Fund Claims Process

While the pre-trial discovery and motion processes were proceeding in both federal and state court, there were claims procedures ongoing that provided at least some interim relief for plaintiffs who had been economically injured. Immediately following the spill, Exxon instituted a claims procedure that made certain payments to fishermen and others who had been damaged financially. In addition, certain plaintiffs, including native corporations, obtained compensation from the Trans-Alaska Pipeline Liability Fund (TAPL Fund), which was established by federal statute in order to make a maximum of $100 million per oil spill available to victims. The native Alaskan corporations collectively received over $23 million in awards from the TAPL Fund. During the state court trial, one of the major issues was whether Exxon was entitled to offset these TAPL Fund awards against the damages awarded by the state court jury. Generally, under common law jurisprudence, a defendant is not entitled to an offset against a damage award for amounts received by a plaintiff from a collateral source, such as insurance purchased by the plaintiff. However, if the victim receives a payment from insurance purchased by the defendant, this is a non-collateral source and the defendant is entitled to an offset. In the case of the TAPL Fund, the Fund was established by Congressional statute for the benefit of victims, but the financing for the Fund came from Exxon and the other oil companies who were the co-owners of the Alyeska Pipeline Company. Ultimately, the Alaska state court judge decided that the state court jury award could be offset by the TAPL Fund award, and the Alaska Supreme Court affirmed on this issue.

Moreover, Alyeska – the pipeline company responsible for the spill prevention and response plan that failed miserably to either prevent or clean-up the spilled oil – settled in 1993 for approximately $97 million. Of that, about $5.6 million was allocated to three native corporations pursuant to an allocation formula agreed to by all plaintiffs and their counsel, with court supervision.

3. The State Court Trial

Certain native corporations and municipalities tried their property and compensatory damage claims in Alaska state court. Prior to trial, the state court judge dismissed the corporations' punitive damage claims in deference to the federal punitive damage trial.

During the state court trial and after the jury verdict on appeal, Exxon argued that no monetary damages could have resulted from the oiling of the native corporations' lands because the wilderness properties affected had no commercial value. In other words, Exxon argued that the corporations' preservation of their lands in their pristine, natural state was not a use but, rather, a "non-use" that was not compensable under the law. In a lengthy opinion and landmark decision handed down on November 22, 1999, the Alaska Supreme Court rejected Exxon's view, holding that preservation is a compensable lost use, and that a property use need not be pecuniary, commercial or income producing to have a value requiring compensation for its impairment or loss. As noted by the Alaska Supreme Court, the native corporations, who gave up valuable aboriginal claims to a large percentage of Alaska under the Alaska Native Claims Settlement Act (ANCSA) in return for clear title to the lands surrounding their villages, preserved large tracts of land in their unspoiled, wilderness condition in order to enable their native shareholders to practice and maintain their native cultures and traditions of subsistence hunting and fishing. As Congress recognized in enacting another statute, the Alaska National Interests Land Conservation Act (ANILCA): "The continuation of the opportunity for subsistence uses . . . by Alaska Natives on Native lands is essential to Native physical, economic, traditional and cultural existence. . . ." The Alaska Supreme Court found that by impairing the Native Lands preservation use, Exxon injured the Alaska native corporations right and duty to hold the lands in their natural state for the benefit of native shareholders. Going even further, the Alaska Supreme Court observed:

> "[I]n an era marked by worldwide population explosion, and emerging global economy and industrial development into virtually every corner of the earth, it hardly seems unrealistic to recognize the value of preserving wilderness as a valid use in itself, quite apart from any incidental benefit conservation might have in promoting subsistence living and cultural survival."

Chenega Corp., et al. v. Exxon Corp., et al. (Nos. S-7252/7512 (Supreme Court, Alaska 1999)).

In addition to finding that wilderness lands have substantial use values in their natural state, the Alaska Supreme Court also accepted the expert testimony that preservation of the wilderness lands required protection of their ecological systems with biological diversity. The court further found that the evidence supported the theory that there was a loss of confidentiality regarding the archeological sites located on natives lands, and that this loss of confidentiality threatened those sites with future damages since the location of the sites became widely known during the clean-up operations following the oil spill. As clean-up crews worked on the beaches, they either intentionally or inadvertently moved or removed artifacts or destroyed archeological sites through vandalism. In addition, experts testified that oil contamination of wooden artifacts could impair accurate dating through radioactive carbon dating techniques. Even the moving of certain artifacts, as the beaches were washed with high pressure hoses, was found to have impaired or destroyed the archeological context of certain sites. The standard for computing damages to the archeological sites was, therefore, held to include the costs of monitoring, excavating and surveying the affected sites, collecting and curating artifacts, and publishing scholarly papers documenting the work. This ruling is significant because the court accepted and validated the theory that the fear of future harm and vandalism may be reasonable and compensable even as long as it was a reasonable and foreseeable consequence of the disaster, not just speculative or conjectural.

The Alaska Supreme Court reversed and remanded for trial on one appellate issue raised by the native corporations themselves. The court, in essence, found the jury instructions given by the state court trial judge had been erroneous to the extent that they required the native corporations to prove that they had suffered actual lost uses of federally owned property that had been selected by them but title to which had not actually been transferred. Following the oil spill, Congress enacted the Oil Pollution Act of 1990 ("OPA90") containing one section (Section 8301) providing that "[s]olely for the purpose of bringing claims that arise from the discharge of oil, the Congress confirms that all right, title and interest of the United States" in lands validly selected by the Alaska native corporations "are deemed to have vested in the respective corporations as of March 23, 1989", the day prior to the disaster. The Alaska Supreme Court found that, by requiring the native corporations to prove actual lost uses by them of these selected properties, the trial court was, in effect, directing a verdict against the native corporations since the native corporations had no greater right to the use of these federally-owned lands than other members of the public. In reversing, the Alaska Supreme Court found that the language chosen by Congress was more consistent with the actual conveyance of an interest in land or an assignment of a right beyond mere "standing". The court reasoned that it would have made little sense for Congress to have granted the native corporations "standing" to sue for injuries to federal lands while, at the same time, knowing that the potential claims of the native corporations were too speculative to sustain a finding of actionable injury under *Lujan v. Defenders of Wildlife*, 504 U.S. 555 (1992), where the US Supreme Court rejected the argument that the citizen-sent provisions of the Endangered Species Act created a "procedural right" to governmental compliance. The Supreme Court found in *Lujan* that, for an environmental group or anyone else to have standing to sue, it must have sustained a concrete injury under Art. III of the US Constitution, which limits standing to sue in US courts to an actual "case or controversy", rather than abstract, speculative or procedural injuries.

4. Technique for Handling and Analysis of Documentary Evidence

The *Exxon Valdez Oil Spill* litigation required handling and analysis of vast quantities of documentation. These efforts were greatly facilitated by judicious application of computer technology. The work naturally fell into two categories based on the character of the documents: (a) legal documents submitted by all parties, including pleadings, briefs, motion papers, discovery requests and responses, etc.; (b) factual documents researched by plaintiffs and produced by defendants as evidence in support of plaintiffs' claims.

The handling of the legal documents was greatly facilitated by an agreement reached early in the litigation whereby all parties (except federal and state governmental plaintiffs) served legal documents on paper and also on electronic storage media (floppy disks) in an agreed upon computer readable format (WordPerfect word processor format). Plaintiffs then contracted with an electronic bulletin board vendor and established an electronic library of all legal documents filed in a secure but remotely accessible bulletin board. These arrangements preceded the now widespread accessibility of World Wide Web storage sites; however, plaintiffs used a remote data storage and retrieval model that has now been widely adopted on the Internet. This allowed all plaintiffs, in firms spread out across the country, to have ready access to all legal documents created.

However, this procedure also allowed for advanced computer-assisted analysis of the legal documents of opposing parties. Each side frequently submitted massive documents containing sprawling information. Plaintiffs designed several proprietary computer and database tools which allowed the vast amounts of data dispersed throughout these documents to be culled, organized and sorted for much faster analysis. Without such assistance, the efforts to determine what witnesses to depose, which evidence to research, and which issues to focus on would have proceeded much less efficiently.

The factual documents researched and collected rapidly grew into the millions of pages. A few central databases were created, storing as much of the useful information found in the evidence as could be identified. Because of the economics of digital image processing at the time, the decision was made to refrain from creating digital images of all evidence, but instead to identify the most useful evidence first. Today, digital imaging is much less expensive, and, in many cases, is feasible even before the wheat has been separated from the chaff. Obviously, the benefits of handling, copying and transporting vast quantifies of documents on a few Compact Disks (CD-ROMs) are enormous.

As trial was nearing and the best evidence had been identified, all parties and the court agreed upon implementing a courtroom-wide high-technology multimedia evidence display system. All documentary evidence had been digitally transferred onto CD-ROMs, all videotaped testimony had been referenced and indexed, and all summary evidence of charts and graphs had been prepared in multimedia format. When the jury walked into the wired courtroom, they were greeted by a system of oversized computer monitors set up for viewing from the jury box, from the witness stand, from the bench, and from the plaintiffs' and defendants' tables. Everything but physical evidence was brought up on the monitors, and in some instances, paper copies were also circulated. The *Exxon Valdez* courtroom was one of the first to be wired in the manner made famous by the criminal trial of O.J. Simpson over a year later. It allowed documents to be called up instantaneously, specific excerpts of videotaped testimony to be played on demand, and it allowed each side to have as steady and seamless presentation as possible.

III. THE *BHOPAL* CASE

The history of the litigation and claims process following the Bhopal Gas Disaster of December 2-3, 1984 exemplifies in many respects, how the complex procedural and jurisdictional issues arising from a major catastrophe can result in disastrous delays in the providing of compensation to victims who are in desperate need of help. If the maxim that "justice delayed is justice denied" is correct, then the *Bhopal* case is a prime example.

1. Factual and Procedural History

Fifteen years ago, on December 3, 1984, a deadly gas leak from Union Carbide's facility killed at least 7,000 people in Bhopal, India and grievously injured several hundred thousand. Independent estimates by the Indian Council of Medical Research (ICMR) and the International Medical Commission on Bhopal suggest that approximately 250,000 continue to suffer from permanent disability and chronic illnesses as a result of exposure to the methyl isocyanate gas which leaked from Union Carbide's plant. Given the enormity of its toll in human lives and suffering, the Bhopal disaster has sometimes been called the "Hiroshima of the Chemical Industry" and is generally characterized as the worst peacetime environmental disaster in history.

Following the disaster, some 145 suits filed in various US courts on behalf of 186,000 individual victims of the catastrophe were consolidated by the Judicial Panel on Multidistrict Litigation and scheduled to be heard before Judge John Keenan in the Southern District of New York. The victims and their lawyers, both in India and the US, viewed the US legal system as having obvious procedural advantages over the Indian court system, to say nothing of the greater damages generally awarded by US juries. On March 25, 1985, however, the Indian Parliament enacted the Bhopal Gas Disaster Act, which directed the Indian government to exercise its *parens patriae* authority to represent the victims in claims for compensation in foreign or domestic courts. Art. 9 of the Act also enabled the Indian Government to establish or frame an administrative scheme to register and process claims for compensation arising from the Disaster. Art. 6 of the Bhopal Act provided for the establishment of an officer, to be known as the Commissioner, to discharge its functions and powers under the Act "for the welfare of the victims of the Bhopal gas leak disaster." The purpose of this legislation was to supercede the role of private attorneys in representation of the Bhopal gas victims and to provide centralized, integrated decision-making and control for effective litigation of the claims against Union Carbide. By way of rationale, proponents of the Act maintained that the gas victims were under a legal disability insofar as they lacked the resources to retain private counsel in the absence of any contingency-fee mechanism under Indian law, and that it was a perfectly legitimate exercise of sovereign power under international law for a state to represent, as an aspect of its protective jurisdiction, the interests of its injured nationals. The proponents also argued that meaningful redress and compensation for the victims of the Bhopal disaster could only be obtained if the full might of the multinational corporation were challenged with all the resources at the disposal of the Indian state apparatus. Unfortunately, while the theory may have been theoretically sound, the implementation proved to be woefully inadequate.

Based on the Bhopal Act, the Indian Government filed suit against Union Carbide on April 8, 1985, alleging counts of negligence, strict liability, absolute liability, breach of warranty and misrepresentation. On May 12, 1986, Judge Keenan conditionally dismissed the consolidated action on the grounds that India was the more appropriate forum for the resolution of this litigation. *In Re: Union Carbide Corp. Gas Plant Disaster at Bhopal, India in December 1984*, 634 F. Supp. 842, 867 (S.D.N.Y. 1986). This dismissal was conditioned upon Union Carbide's "consent to submit to the jurisdiction of the courts of India", which was not fully complied with. The Court of Appeals affirmed Judge Keenan's dismissal, noting again the condition that Union Carbide must fully submit to Indian court jurisdiction. *In Re: Union Carbide Corp. Gas Plant Disaster at Bhopal, India in December 1984*, 809 F.2d 195 (2d Cir. 1987), *cert. denied*, 484 U.S. 871, 108 S.Ct. 199, 98 L.Ed.2d 150 (1987). Consequently, the Indian Government filed suit against Union Carbide in Bhopal District Court on September 5, 1986.

Litigation continued in India for more than two years thereafter without even reaching the commencement of pretrial discovery. Civil litigation in Indian courts is subject to delays of 20 years or more as a result of overburdened dockets and an outmoded procedural system allowing for multiple interlocutory appeals on virtually any decision made by the trial court. The sheer scale of the *Bhopal* litigation, perhaps not surprisingly, proved overwhelming for the Indian legal system. By the time the controversy reached the Supreme Court of India on the issue of whether interim relief assessed against Union Carbide on behalf of the victims was appropriate, the need for some time-bound resolution of the litigation in order to guarantee immediate relief to the victims of the tragedy had become very pressing. Consequently, on February 14, 1989, after nearly four months of oral and written argument, Chief Justice Rajinder S. Pathak interrupted the proceedings to announce that he felt, in light of "the enormity of suffering occasioned by the Bhopal gas disaster and the pressing urgency to provide immediate and substantial relief to the victims," that the case was "preeminently fit for overall settlement." *Union Carbide Corp. v. Union of India*, 1 S.C.C. 674, 675 (1989). He then ordered Union Carbide to pay $470 million in damages. In its decision of October 1991, the Indian Supreme Court approved the settlement, but modified its terms and conditions including a reinstatement of criminal charges against Union Carbide and its former CEO, Warren Anderson. *Union Carbide Corp. v. Union of India*, Review Petition Nos. 229 and 623-24 of 1989, 70 (1991). The Court reasoned that the Bhopal Act and the civil settlement flowing from it did not deal with any claims or rights arising from Union Carbide's criminal liability.

After the Supreme Court rendered its decision, criminal charges against Union Carbide and Warren Anderson were renewed in the Bhopal District Court. In March 1992, Judge Sharma issued an arrest warrant for Warren Anderson and gave lawyers for Union Carbide a month in which to appear for trial. Neither of the parties presented themselves in court and Union Carbide's official spokesperson stated that the Company would flatly refuse to submit to the jurisdiction of India's criminal courts. Summonses served on Union Carbide through the US Department of Justice and Interpol were ignored, and the Company and Warren Anderson were declared "proclaimed absconders" by the Bhopal District Court. The designation of "proclaimed absconder" is a term of art in Indian law which is equivalent to "fugitive from justice" in the American legal system.

2. The Alien Tort Claims Act Complaint

On November 15, 1999, the Bhopal victims and five of their organizations filed a class action complaint under the Alien Tort Claims Act in federal court in New York before Judge Keenan, alleging violations of international law and fundamental human rights for the unlawful, reckless and depraved indifference to human life in the design, operation and maintenance of the Bhopal facility. As set forth in the complaint, Union Carbide intentionally failed to install safety devices and procedures in the Bhopal plant, which were installed in Union Carbide's sister plant in Institute, West Virginia.

3. The Claims Process

On February 3, 1991, the first of eight tribunals created to disburse the settlement proceeds began functioning in Bhopal. However, it was unable to do any effective work until June 22, 1991 when the Indian Government finally issued guidelines regarding the quantum of payments to each category of victim. The registry of victims was narrowly restricted and until the Indian Supreme Court stepped in with an order on December 10, 1998, children and other categories of victims were excluded. Based on a fairly arbitrary system of classification derived from some of the initial surveys conducted by the Indian Commission on Medical Research, the Government specified only seven categories of victims as eligible for compensation: death; permanent total or partial disability; temporary total or partial disability; injury of utmost severity; loss of belongings; and loss of livestock. No compensation was provided for loss of business or for pain and suffering. Theoretically at least, the maximum compensation for deaths was approximately $7,500. Loss of belongings would be compensated up to $375 and loss of livestock up to $250. In practice, the amounts awarded were much lower. For example, until January 1993, almost the whole first year after these claims courts were established, only claims arising out of deaths were heard. Of these, 1,710 claims were decided, of which 1,152 (67%) were rejected. This bleak picture was further complicated by the fact that the Indian Government made no effort to provide legal counsel for the victims in order to pursue claims for compensation before the tribunals and most, if not all, claimants appeared *pro se*. Essentially, each claimant was required to provide evidence or proof, by medical certificate, government classification under the ICMR registry or postmortem records, that they belonged to a particular category. Awards were then made within the range of maximum to minimum allotted to each category of injury.

The October 1991 judgment of the Supreme Court of India had directed the Government to establish at least 40 claims tribunals in Bhopal by February 1992. According to official records, however, only five claims tribunals were opened by that date and another thirteen more were created in July 1992. An additional twelve were established in late January 1993. In addition to the 30 claims tribunals, five administrative courts of appeal also functioned while the Welfare Commissioner presided over a Revision Court which decided only those cases where it was determined that compensation should not have been awarded or was made in excess. Nine years after the disaster in 1993, most victims had received nothing except the Rs. 200 offered them by the Indian Government as interim relief. The claims courts had decided less than 5% of all claims and the average compensation had been a meager $2,500 in cases of death. For serious injuries, with total and permanent disability, the compensation ranged from $500 to $1,250. This standard of compensation compares very poorly when compared to the average awarded by Indian consumer tribunals in personal injury cases, and constitutes less than half the amount awarded to serious injury claimants under the Indian Fatal Accidents Act.

Present-day estimates by non-governmental organizations documenting the medical and environmental aspects of the Bhopal Disaster indicate that over

90% of claimants have received less than $400 from the claims process in India. Furthermore, no attempts have been made to undertake an environmental clean-up of the plant site and surrounding environs of the Bhopal disaster. Recent soil and water sample tests conducted by an independent British laboratory for Greenpeace and certain victims' organizations indicate massive contamination of soil and drinking water around the Union Carbide facility in Bhopal. For example, the Greenpeace report states that water samples taken from the Bhopal site contained carbon tetrachloride, a carcinogenic chemical, which exceeded maximum tolerance limits established by the World Health Organization by 1,705 times.

IV. CONCLUSION

The tortured procedural history of the *Bhopal* litigation demonstrates the need for an effective international dispute resolution tribunal, such as the Permanent Court of Arbitration, to resolve mass tort disaster claims in an efficient and expeditious manner. The US legal system, even with the broad jurisdictional provisions of the Alien Tort Claims Act and the recent successful class settlement with the Swiss Banks in the Holocaust-related litigation, cannot fully obviate the need for an international tribunal where the merits of a case can be directly addressed without extended procedural maneuvering and *forum non conveniens* analysis. The *Exxon Valdez* and *Bhopal* litigations also teach us that, however well intentioned, governments should stick to what they do best, which is to handle the criminal investigation and prosecution, as well as the governmental and public damage claims, resulting from a mass tort disaster. However, regarding the private damage claims of individuals, corporations and property owners, private counsel experienced in complex litigation should be permitted to pursue those claims in the appropriate forum on a contingent fee or other basis, without preemption by the governmental entities concerned. Private counsel can successfully organize themselves and their client groups into an effective organization to pursue the discovery and trial of the private claims and to coordinate with the governmental attorneys. State of the art document storage and retrieval systems, including the use of CD-ROM and the internet, can be effectively used to organize and present a complex litigation.

Finally, once a common fund is established by way of settlement or award, the allocation and claims process must be sufficiently flexible, avoiding the imposition of reasonably low standard of proof for any individual claimants, so that the common fund can be distributed to the intended victims as expeditiously as possible.

Arbitration Principles Prove Effective in Resolving Holocaust Bank Claims*

*Lucy Reed***

I. INTRODUCTION

In the spring of 1997, the Independent Committee of Eminent Persons ("ICEP") chaired by Paul Volcker, the Swiss Bankers Association and the Swiss Federal Banking Commission announced the creation of the "Claims Resolution Tribunal for Dormant Bank Accounts in Switzerland." The Claims Resolution Tribunal (known as the "CRT") was launched in 1998.

The primary mission of the Claims Resolution Tribunal, with which I have had the privilege to be involved, is a profoundly important and historical one: to locate the rightful owners of assets deposited with Swiss banks before World War II by foreigners who later became the victims of Nazi persecution and hence unable to reclaim those assets.

One needs to know several things, beyond the incomprehensible evil of the Holocaust itself, to understand how this situation came to pass: first, under Swiss law, there is no escheat of the assets in inactive bank accounts to the state, as there is in the United States; second, under Swiss law, there is a 10-year document retention period for bank documents, with the exception perhaps of the original account-opening document; and, third, Swiss banks follow very strict practices concerning confidentiality and proof of inherited rights to private bank accounts. It also helps to know, to put the situation into perspective, albeit ironic perspective, that private Swiss banking originated

---

* This article is based on a talk delivered to the AAA Corporate Counsel Committee in New York on January 13, 1999, that was printed in a publication of Transnational Publishers, Inc., Ardsley, New York. It is reprinted by permission. The views expressed herein are strictly the author's personal views.

** Member, Freshfields International Arbitration Group and Public International Law Group, New York; since July 1998, co-director of the Claims Resolution Tribunal for Dormant Swiss Bank Accounts in Switzerland, and presently Policy Director.

early in this century to help clients protect their assets from dictators and war disruption.

The purpose of this article is not to address the primary mission of the Claims Resolution Tribunal. Others have already done so and many more will do so in the future.

The limited purpose of this article, instead, is to describe how the basic principles of international commercial arbitration provided certain foundation stones of this unique multiple claims resolution process. These underpinnings are evident not just in the Rules of Procedure for the Claims Resolution Process ("CRT Rules"), but also in the evolving practice and jurisprudence of the Claims Resolution Tribunal. An unexpected benefit of participating in the CRT has been the opportunity to observe, and better appreciate, the inherent and enduring value of the most basic arbitration principles: why we need them, why they work in widely varying circumstances, and why arbitration without them can be fragile business indeed.

Three introductory caveats:

- First, there obviously is no equating the circumstances underlying unclaimed Holocaust-era bank accounts and typical commercial contract disputes. The point is that the arbitral building blocks must be the same if the arbitral process is to be – and appear to all involved to be – fair, credible and final.

- Second, the "Arbitral Principles" presented in this article do not appear in order of importance. By far the most important are those principles involving impartiality, independence and neutrality.

- Third, as one who served as a counsel to the Claims Resolution Tribunal, I cannot address many issues, either because they involve cases under adjudication or policies in process. In a related vein, I do not want to appear to be criticizing any aspect of the CRT process: anyone who has been involved in negotiating a claims resolution process, or even an arbitration clause, knows that compromises are always necessary.

II. BACKGROUND TO THE CLAIMS RESOLUTION TRIBUNAL PROCESS

1. Publication of Accounts and Claim Filings

In May 1996, the Swiss banks, in cooperation with major Jewish organizations, established the Independent Commission of Eminent Persons (known as "ICEP") to oversee a comprehensive audit to identify all accounts that could have belonged to victims of Nazi persecution. All the major accounting firms played some role in the audit. A non-financial aspect of the audit is to match Account Holders (and holders of Power of Attorney, who often, for example as Jews, were the beneficial owners) to various databases – all uncomputerized – of victims of Nazi persecution. ICEP announced in January 1999 that the audit was to conclude in March 1999, after which ICEP would publish a final report.

By 1997, the Swiss banks and ICEP auditors had identified 5,570 accounts that apparently had been opened by foreigners (non-Swiss nationals and non-Swiss residents) and remained dormant since May 9, 1945. (The process also identified another approximately 7,500 dormant accounts opened by Swiss nationals and residents, which are being handled directly by the Swiss banks.) On July 23 and October 29, 1997, the Swiss Bankers Association published – worldwide – lists of the Account Holder names and places of residence for each of the 5,570 accounts. The lists did not include the name of the Swiss bank holding the account or the amount in the account. The October list, unlike the July list, indicated which amounts have a current reported balance of CHF 100 or less. (This article does not refer to any lists of accounts that may be published after the October 1997 list or to procedures related to any such additional accounts.)

The publication invited persons who believed themselves entitled to the accounts to contact Ernst & Young offices in several countries or by Internet. Ernst & Young then sent out Claim Form packages and provided claim filing assistance on toll-free lines. The Claim Form sought information and, when available, documentation concerning the identity of the Account Holder and the relationship between the claimant and the Account Holder. Ernst & Young accepted completed Claim Forms, numbered the claims and created a database.

Ernst & Young then sent each Claim Form to the Swiss bank holding the account for a first review of a possible match. Where the bank was satisfied that information connected the claimant and the Account Holder, the bank authorized its identity and the amount in the account to the claimant. Where the bank found no such connection, the bank sent the file back to Ernst & Young. In all cases, Ernst & Young transmitted the files to the Claims Resolution Tribunal.

2. Results of Publication and Filing

As of January 1999, Ernst & Young had received some 9,500 claims against the 5,570 published foreign accounts. In actuality, these 9,500 claims were made on only some 2,500 – approximately 45 percent – of the published accounts. The supposition is that no claims were made on the other 55 percent of the published accounts either because the amount was very small (per the October list) or because no heirs of the Account Holders survived or saw the publication.

There are some 7,200 claimants behind the 9,500 Claim Forms, as several filed on multiple accounts. Most of the 2,500 claimed-upon accounts were claimed by several claimants: the average is four claims per account. The most claims on one account, which was opened by an Account Holder with a common surname, total 71.

The claimants come from 27 countries, filing Claim Forms in 20 different languages. In terms of demographics, the major claimant nationalities are US (20 percent), German (12 percent), French (12 percent), Israeli (nine percent) and Argentinean (six percent). The major claimant languages are English (37 percent), German (19 percent), French (14 percent), Spanish (nine percent) and Hebrew (six percent).

Upon receipt of the Claim Forms from Ernst & Young, the Swiss banks disclosed additional information – their identity and the amount in the relevant accounts – in approximately 3,000 of the 9,500 claims. This bears emphasis: in approximately 30 percent of the claims, the Swiss banks voluntarily disclosed formerly secret information to claimants.

3. Monetary Values

The total current balance of the 5,570 published foreign dormant accounts, as reported by the banks, is approximately CHF 72 million. The total current balance of the 2,500 claimed-upon accounts is CHF 66 million

This is, however, a misleadingly low figure. ICEP recognizes that, although savings and other cash accounts in Swiss banks were generally non-interest bearing early in the century, victims of Nazi persecution certainly did not intend to leave their assets in non-interest bearing accounts for more than 50 years. Nor did such victims intend to have their assets depleted indefinitely by the deduction of bank fees for private accounts, e.g. fees charged for not mailing statements.

Accordingly, the Board of Trustees of the Independent Claims Resolution Foundation committed to issue Guidelines to the CRT on how to estimate and add interest and previously deducted bank fees to Awards, based on the recommendations of an independent expert panel chaired by Henry Kaufman. The Board of Trustees has indicated its intention that these Guidelines apply only to successful claimants to accounts of victims of Nazi persecution or other wartime persecution. Whatever the final numbers, application of the Guidelines will multiply the current balance of the accounts substantially. (The Guidelines had not yet been issued at the time of writing this article.)

III. THE CLAIMS RESOLUTION TRIBUNAL: ARBITRATION PRINCIPLES

1. *Why an Arbitration Tribunal?*

Arbitration Principle 1
Arbitration Is the Answer When the Parties Cannot Resolve the Disputed Matters Themselves for Legal, Commercial or Political Reasons.

In discussing the Claims Resolution Tribunal, the first question that presents itself is: Why an arbitration tribunal at all? Why use arbitration to resolve disputes or, more accurately, to determine ownership – whether or not disputed – of dormant Swiss bank accounts?

The political reality, if not the ends of justice alone, was that impartial third-parties had to step into the relationship between the Swiss banks and their clients – really those clients' heirs – because the banks were not perceived to have dealt fairly with those clients and heirs. There were many publicized examples of rigid treatment by the banks of heirs of Holocaust survivors, for example bank demands for death certificates for parents who died in the concentration camps. Furthermore, the two bank-driven programs to identify and return accounts to Holocaust victims, after World War II and in 1962, obviously were neither thorough nor reliable. In sum, despite the Swiss banks' extraordinary cooperation with the ICEP process, in which the Swiss banking community has invested hundreds of millions of dollars, the fact remains that any payment program controlled by the banks would fall short in world public opinion.

Therefore, ICEP, the Swiss Bankers Association and the Swiss Federal Banking Commission established an arbitration tribunal to determine claims to the foreign dormant accounts. By definition, such a tribunal would provide the independence, impartiality and objectivity that both the world Jewish community and Swiss banks required.

2. Governance and Constitution of the Claims Resolution Tribunal

Arbitration Principle 2
For Actual and Apparent Credibility, an Arbitral Tribunal or Panel – Although All Arbitrators Are Impartial – Should Be Party-Balanced.

The Board of Trustees of the Independent Claims Resolution Foundation ("Board of Trustees"), which is itself comprised of Mr. Volcker and representatives of the World Jewish Congress and the Swiss Government, selected sixteen eminent senior Arbitrators for the Claims Resolution Tribunal. All serve on a part-time basis.

All of the arbitrators are strictly neutral and their composition is well-balanced: one-fourth are Israeli, one-fourth are Swiss, and one-half are from third countries. The Chairman is Hans Michael Riemer, a Jewish Swiss law professor and judge. The Israeli arbitrators are: Judge Hadassah Ben-Itto, David Friedmann, Doron Shorrer, and Tsevi Tal. The Swiss arbitrators, in addition to the Chairman, are: Robert Briner, Franz Kellerhals, Hans Nater, and Luc Thévenoz. The other arbitrators are: Thomas Buergenthal (USA), L. Yves Fortier (Canada), Lord Higgins (UK), Howard M. Holtzmann (USA), Andrew J. Jacovides (Cyprus), Roberts B. Owen (USA), and William W. Park (USA).

Arbitration Principle 3
For Actual and Apparent Credibility, an Arbitral Tribunal Should Be Geographically Neutral.

Rather than creating a new administrative entity, the Board of Trustees requested an eminent Swiss law firm, Schellenberg & Haissly, to serve as Secretariat. This strategy was aimed at saving start-up time and infrastructure expenditures, and also at avoiding the self-perpetuating tendencies of international institutions. However, the Swiss venue of the Claims Resolution Tribunal has created for many the perception of affiliation with one side, the Swiss banks, which has led to criticism of the claims resolution process.

Arbitration Principle 4
Modern Arbitrators and Their Professional Assistants, to Be Efficient, Should Take Advantage of the Latest Information Technology.

The Secretariat, as of January 1999, had some 45 full-time staff working in four teams in Zurich and Geneva. There are some 30 lawyers (known as "legal secretaries," in Continental parlance), many of whom are young litigators generously seconded by eminent law firms, including Debevoise & Plimpton, Vinson & Elkins, Herbert Smith, Freshfields, Hogan & Hartson and Perkins Coie. The Secretariat also includes paralegals, translators, clerical secretaries and administrators.

The CRT works officially in English, German, French and Italian. The legal secretaries, who have come from some dozen countries, also work in Hebrew, Spanish, Portuguese, Dutch, Russian, Polish, Croatian and Czech. The staff translators, contracting out as necessary, work in the other claimant languages.

The Secretariat puts modern information technology to full use. The legal secretaries draft all memoranda and decision documents for the arbitrators directly on the computer, using carefully-created template documents (in all four working languages) to maximize uniformity of format for claimants. They also have developed a website (http://www.crt.ch), created claims databases, customized claims management software, and tailored genealogy software for creating family trees. The legal secretaries communicate internally and with the arbitrators by e-mail, and conduct both legal and factual research on the Internet.

IV. THE CLAIMS RESOLUTION PROCESS AND RULES OF PROCEDURE

Arbitration Principle 5
Arbitration, Which Is Consensual, Should Be Clearly Distinguished from Administrative and Other Nonbinding Dispute Resolution Mechanisms.

There are three basic procedures under CRT jurisdiction: 1) Initial Screening, 2) Fast Track arbitration, and 3) Ordinary Procedure arbitration. In Initial Screening cases, also known as "non-disclosure cases," a sole arbitrator reviews a bank decision not to disclose its identity and the account amount to a claimant. In Fast Track and Ordinary Procedure cases, also known as "disclosure cases," sole arbitrators or three-arbitrator Claims Panels determine entitlement to accounts for which the banks have disclosed the additional information to one or more claimants. Parties to Fast Track and Ordinary Procedure cases must execute arbitration agreements, called Claims Resolution Agreements. Of the approximately 9,500 claims filed with the CRT, some 6,500 are Initial Screening/non-disclosure cases, and some 3,000 are disclosure cases.

Fast Track arbitration, contrary to its nomenclature, is not an expedited full-scale arbitration. A Fast Track arbitration is a disclosure case in which the bank offers to pay the account balance to a claimant whom the bank considers entitled. Although Fast Track is a settlement process, the CRT Rules nonetheless require a sole arbitrator to conduct at least a limited review of the file to make certain determinations as to the validity of the claim.

Ordinary Procedure arbitration – although "extraordinary" in that it is the smallest category of CRT cases – is the closest thing in CRT jurisprudence to ordinary commercial arbitration. A sole arbitrator – or if the account balance exceeds CHF 3,000, a three-arbitrator Claims Panel – issues procedural orders to build the file, makes a full review of the claim and all the evidence, and ultimately resolves any disputed entitlement before making an Award. However, compared to ordinary commercial arbitration, CRT Ordinary Procedure is streamlined and expeditious. The CRT Rules envision that cases will be decided on the papers alone in all but exceptional cases.

The Initial Screening procedure warrants particular mention because, although it comprises by far the largest category of CRT cases, it is not an arbitral process. Initial Screening is, in effect, the *de novo* review by a sole arbitrator of the bank's decision not to disclose its identity or the amount in the account to a claimant. Initial Screening claimants have not signed an arbitration agreement with the relevant bank and, indeed, at the Initial Screening stage do not even know the identity of the relevant bank. Only if the sole arbitrator orders disclosure would the claimant and the bank sign a Claims Resolution Agreement.

Initial Screening, which is perhaps most analogous to an administrative review of the bank non-disclosure decision, is an unprecedented form of multiple claims resolution. Some feel that to combine Initial Screening with the true arbitral processes of the CRT (Fast Track and Ordinary Procedure) has caused confusion for the parties and the public.

Arbitration Principle 6
Arbitration Procedures Must Be Flexible, to Meet the Needs at Hand.

The most distinguishing characteristic of CRT arbitration, *qua* arbitration, is the relaxed standard of proof. This "rough justice" standard of proof, which is the very heart of this historic process, appears in Art. 22 of the CRT Rules:

> "The claimant must show that it is plausible in light of all the circumstances that he or she is entitled, in whole or in part, to the dormant account. The Sole Arbitrators or the Claims Panels shall assess all information submitted by the parties or otherwise available to them. They shall at all times bear in mind the difficulties of proving a claim after the destruction of the Second World War and the Holocaust and the long time that has lapsed since the opening of these dormant accounts.
>
> A finding of plausibility requires, *inter alia*,
>
> (i) that all documents and other information have been submitted by the claimant regarding the relationship between the claimant and the published account holder that can reasonably be expected to be produced in view of the particular circumstances, including, without limitation, the history of the claimant's family and whether or not the published

account holder was a victim of Nazi persecution; and

(ii) that no reasonable basis exists to conclude that fraud or forgery affect the claim or evidence submitted; or that other persons may have an identical or better claim to the dormant account."

This fair and realistic standard of proof, as with the expeditious and informal case-handling procedures, is the result of the Board of Trustees' careful tailoring of arbitral procedures to the unique CRT caseload. The CRT simply could not have functioned with full contentious proceedings or a standard burden of proof.

Arbitration Principle 7
Good Arbitrators, and Their Professional Assistants, Must Be Willing to Master the Facts.

Although Initial Screening is not an arbitral procedure, one aspect of the process merits analysis in relation to commercial arbitration – the necessity of mastering complex facts. The CRT deals with a category of facts not common in commercial arbitration, namely personal stories that can be moving and painful, but the fact-mastery skills are the same.

Art. 10(3) of the CRT Rules requires the sole arbitrator to order disclosure unless the claimant fails two minimal tests:

> "The Sole Arbitrator shall order that the name of the bank and the amount held in the dormant account be disclosed to the claimant, unless he or she determines in the initial screening that
>
> (i) the claimant has not submitted any information on his or her entitlement to the dormant account, or
>
> (ii) if it is apparent that the claimant is not entitled to the dormant account.

The test, in practical terms, is whether a claimant in Initial Screening has provided *prima facie* evidence of plausible entitlement under the relaxed standard of proof, or whether the claim is "plausibly plausible."

Under Art. 10(3)(i), "information on entitlement to the dormant account" would include personal information regarding the Account Holder, for example a birthdate or home address, a signature sample matching that in the bank file, or a family story about the Account Holder's having had funds in a Swiss bank. The fact that the claimant and the Account Holder have the same surname is generally not sufficient "information on entitlement."

Under Art. 10(3)(ii), the claimant must demonstrate some connection to the Account Holder. For example, an arbitrator would deny a claim under Art. 10(3)(ii) when it is apparent, on the basis of information provided by the claimant, that he or she is the heir of a Mr. Josef Smit, but the bank file shows that the Account Holder is a different Josef Smit. The classic example is that of a claimant who proves a connection to a Josef Smit who was born in 1925, claiming on an account opened by a Josef Smit who was born in 1900.

The Initial Screening test is fact-driven. Most Claim Forms contain hand-written personal stories, and attach personal documentation in many languages and often in fragile condition: passports, birth certificates, death certificates, marriage records, photographs, deeds, wills, letters, postcards, and school records. The materials are compiled by lay persons, usually elderly, without counsel. The legal secretaries and arbitrators have to piece the stories and documents together, both within a claim file and between the multiple claim files for each account. They have become, not surprisingly, experts on drafting family trees and spotting obscure connections.

Arbitration Principle 8
Arbitrators Must Treat All Parties Equally, to Ensure Both Actual and Apparent Due Process.

Given the factual complexity of most CRT cases, it is fortunate that the Secretariat and arbitrators face comparatively few complex substantive law issues. To date, the most difficult substantive issues concern conflicts of inheritance law, which arise in Ordinary Procedure cases where there are competing claims by multiple alleged heirs from different countries. To ensure that all claimants are treated fairly under their own law, and at the same time equally, requires particular care.

That there are multiple claimants to almost all accounts has also led to complex procedural issues. Art. 20 of the CRT Rules requires joinder of "relevant claims," which necessarily leads to intricate procedural orders and distribution of documentation (which must be translated) to parties in many countries. Whether or not there are multiple claimants filing on an account, it is common for individual claimants to identify other heirs in their Claim Forms and to offer to represent them. In such cases, the CRT has to obtain Powers of Attorney, valid under applicable law to protect all involved, and make arrangements for the additional heirs to become separate claimants by executing Claims Resolution Agreements.

Arbitration Principle 9
Equality of Representation, and Good Representation, Assists the Arbitrators and Assists the Arbitration Process.

There is a necessary nuance to Arbitration Principle 9 in the Claims Resolution Tribunal. The complexity of substantive and procedural legal issues is compounded by the reality that the claimants, in all but rare cases, do not have counsel. The banks generally have inside or outside counsel. A significant part of the legal secretaries' responsibility is to assist claimants to understand the CRT processes and that they are able to present their cases effectively. To this end, the Board of Trustees insisted on toll free numbers or collect call arrangements between the Secretariat and all 27 countries in which claimants reside. In assisting the claimant community, the CRT lawyers, of course, must remain on the appropriate side of the line of neutrality.

Arbitration Principle 10
Arbitrator Neutrality, Both Actual and Apparent, Is the Backbone of International Arbitration.

Any discussion of due process and equal treatment is not complete without consideration of arbitrator impartiality.

The CRT arbitrators follow the highest possible standards. Art. 8 of the CRT Rules allows an arbitrator to be challenged "if circumstances exist that give rise to legitimate doubts concerning his or her independence or integrity," and the CRT adopted International Bar Association-type ethics rules.

However, a practical problem arose early on: all private Swiss banks are parties in the CRT and, not surprisingly, several arbitrators have direct or indirect connections with the banks. With a caseload exceeding 9,500 claims, and the need to have Claims Panels balanced for both nationality and language, automatic recusal for apparent as well as actual conflicts was unworkable. Accordingly, the CRT adopted a tiered approach: 1) in any case of direct conflict, i.e., where an arbitrator personally represents a Swiss bank, the arbitrator recuses himself or herself without any disclosure and waiver option; 2) in Fast Track and Ordinary Procedure cases where there is an apparent conflict, i.e., an arbitrator's firm represents a bank, the arbitrator discloses the connection in his or her Declaration of Independence, which is sent to all parties; and 3) in Initial Screening cases, rather than send a Declaration of Independence to hundreds of non-arbitrating parties, the Chairman does not appoint any arbitrator with an apparent conflict. To date, there have been no challenges filed.

V. CONCLUSION

Having opened with a discussion of the Tribunal's origins, an appropriate conclusion is a brief status report.

As of January 1999, the Claims Resolution Tribunal had received 9,268 claims, 6,437 of which were Initial Screening cases and 2,798 of which were disclosure cases (1,087 classified as Fast Track and 373 as Ordinary Procedure, with classifications in other cases pending). Approximately 2,500 Initial Screening decisions had been rendered, with the arbitrators disagreeing with the banks and ordering disclosure in some 10 percent of the cases. The arbitrators had rendered approximately 100 Fast Track Awards and 5 Ordinary Procedure Awards. Another approximately 850 Initial Screening cases, 500 Fast Track cases, and 350 Ordinary Procedure cases were in process, meaning that they were under active consideration by the legal secretaries and arbitrators.

Clearly, the Claims Resolution Tribunal has a difficult road to climb. Among other things, it must address the negative public perception caused by early promises – made before it was known how many claims would be filed – from the Swiss Bankers Association and ICEP that the claims resolution process could be completed within one year from publication. However, given its strong foundations – many of which were borrowed from international commercial arbitration – the CRT undoubtedly will accomplish its crucial historic mission in a full, fair and just way.

Resources

Claims Resolution Tribunal Website: http://www.crt.ch

Proceedings of the Swiss Arbitration Association, "The Claims Resolution Process for Dormant Accounts in Switzerland", January 22, 1999, please contact Mrs. Waltraud M. Zepf, Pestalozzi Gmuer & Patry, Löwenstrasse 1, CH-8001 Zurich, Switzerland, wzep@pgpzh.ch.

ANNEXES

ANNEX I

Consolidated Tribunal Rules of Procedure

7 March 1984
(amendment to Tribunal Rule 13)

Definitions

The following definitions apply for the purpose of the Tribunal Rules:

(a) "Algiers Declarations" means the two Declarations of the Government of the Democratic and Popular Republic of Algeria, dated 19 January 1981.

(b) "Arbitral tribunal" means either the Full Tribunal or a Chamber, depending on whichever is seised of a particular case or issue.

(c) "Arbitrating party" means, in a particular case, the party or parties initiating recourse to arbitration (the claimant), or the other party or parties (the respondent). The term "arbitrating party" also means one of the two Governments when, in a particular case, it is a claimant or respondent, or when it refers a dispute or question to the Tribunal pursuant to the Algiers Declarations.

(d) "Chamber" means a panel of three members composed by the President of the Tribunal from among the nine members of the Full Tribunal, pursuant to his powers under Article III, paragraph 1 of the Claims Settlement Declaration.

(e) "Claims Settlement Declaration" means the "Declaration of the Democratic and Popular Republic of Algeria Concerning the Settlement of Claims by the Government of the United States and the Government of the Islamic Republic of Iran", dated 19 January 1981.

(f) "Full Tribunal" means the nine member Tribunal.

(g) "Member" as used in the Tribunal Rules shall have the same meaning as "arbitrator" where used in the UNCITRAL Rules.

(h) "National", "Iran", and the "United States" shall have the same meanings as defined in Article VII of the Claims Settlement Declaration.

(i) "President" means the President of the Tribunal.

(j) "Presiding arbitrator" or "presiding member" means the President of the Tribunal or the Chairman of a Chamber, as the case may be.

(k) "Registrar" means the Registrar of the Tribunal and includes any deputy of, or other person authorized by, the Registrar, the President, or the Full Tribunal to perform a function for which the Registrar is responsible.

(l) "Secretary-General" means the Secretary-General of the Tribunal and includes any deputy of, or other person authorized by, the Secretary-General, the President, or the Full Tribunal to perform a function for which the Secretary-General is responsible.

(m) "Tribunal" means the Iran-United States Claims Tribunal established within the framework of and pursuant to the Algiers Declarations.

(n) "Tribunal Rules" means these Rules, as they may from time to time be modified or supplemented by the Full Tribunal or the two Governments.

(o) "The two Governments" means the Government of the Islamic Republic of Iran and the Government of the United States of America.

(p) "UNCITRAL Arbitration Rules" and "UNCITRAL Rules" mean the Arbitration Rules of the United Nations Commission on International Trade Law which are the subject of Resolution 31/98 adopted by the General Assembly of the United Nations on 15 December 1976.

SECTION I. INTRODUCTORY RULES

Scope of Application

Article 1

1. Within the framework of the Algiers Declarations, the initiation and conduct of proceedings before the arbitral tribunal shall be subject to the following Tribunal Rules which may be modified by the Full Tribunal or the two Governments.

2. These Rules shall govern the arbitration except that where any of these Rules is in conflict with a provision of the law applicable to the arbitration from which the parties cannot derogate, that provision shall prevail.

3. The Claims Settlement Declaration constitutes an agreement in writing by Iran and the United States, on their own behalfs and on behalf of their nationals submitting to arbitration within the framework of the Algiers Declarations and in accordance with the Tribunal Rules.

Notice, Calculation of Periods of Time

Article 2

1. All documents must be filed with the Tribunal. Filing of a document with the Tribunal shall be deemed to have been made when it is physically received by the Registrar.

2. All documents filed in a particular case shall be served upon all arbitrating parties in that case through the Agents. The Registrar shall promptly deliver copies to the offices of each of the two Agents in The Hague, except for a filing Agent. Each Agent shall be responsible for transmitting one copy to each concerned arbitrating party in his country or to the representative designated by each such arbitrating party to receive documents on its behalf.

3. The filing of documents with the Tribunal shall constitute service on all of the other arbitrating parties in the case and shall be deemed to have been received by said arbitrating parties when it is received by the Agent of their Government.

4. Notwithstanding the provisions of paragraphs 1-3 of Article 2, when the arbitral tribunal has so permitted in a particular case, service of written evidence may be effected by actual delivery to the representative of an arbitrating party during a hearing or a pre-hearing conference in that case. The Secretary-General shall make a record of such service which shall be signed by him. A copy of each document so served, together with such record of service, shall be delivered by the Secretary-General to the Registrar after the hearing or pre-hearing conference at which service was so made.

5. The Registrar may refuse to accept any document which is not received within the required time period or which does not comply with the Algiers Declarations or with the Tribunal Rules. Any such refusal by the Registrar is, upon objection by an arbitrating party concerned within thirty days of notification of refusal, subject to review by the arbitral tribunal.

Notes to Article 2

1. For the purposes of calculating a period of time under these Rules, such period shall begin to run on the day following the day when the document is received. If the last day of such period is an official holiday or a non-business day at the seat of the arbitral tribunal, the period is extended until the first business day which follows. Official holidays and non-business days occurring during the running of the period of time are included in calculating the period. The Secretary-General will issue a list of such days.

2. Twenty copies of all documents shall be filed with the Registrar, unless a smaller number is determined by the arbitral tribunal. In the event that there are more than two arbitrating parties in a case, a sufficient number of additional copies shall be filed to permit service on all arbitrating parties in the case. Also, the arbitral tribunal, or the Registrar, may at any time require a party which files a document to submit additional copies.

3. Exhibits and written evidence, other than those annexed to the Statement of Claim or Statement of Defence, shall be submitted in such manner and number of copies as the arbitral tribunal may determine in each case based on the nature and volume of the particular exhibit or written evidence and any other relevant circumstances.

4. Upon the filing of a document, the Registrar shall note on all copies the date received. The Registrar shall issue a receipt to the arbitrating party which filed the document. In all instances in which the Registrar is required to deliver copies to the Agents, he will secure a written receipt of such delivery, which will be kept in the case file and be available for inspection or copying by any arbitrating party in that case.

5. All documents filed with the Registrar are to be submitted on paper 8 1/2 inches × 11 inches or on A-4 size paper (21 cm × 29.5 cm), or on paper no larger than A-4. If a document, exhibit or other written evidence cannot conveniently be reproduced on paper no larger than A-4, it is to be folded to A-4 size, unless the Registrar permits otherwise in special circumstances.

6. Upon filing a Statement of Claim, the Registrar shall assign an identifying number to the claim, and the case shall be assigned to the Full Tribunal, or by lot to a Chamber. Thereafter, all documents filed in the case, including the award, shall have a caption stating:

   (i) the names of the parties,

(ii) the case number assigned by the Registrar, and

(iii) the number of the Chamber seised of the case; otherwise the caption shall state "Full Tribunal."

7. At least two copies in English and two copies in Persian of all documents mentioned in Article 17, Note 3 and filed with the Tribunal shall be manually signed by the arbitrating party submitting them or by its representative. Exhibits and annexes to documents need not be signed. If a document is presented without such signatures, it shall be accepted for filing, but the filing party shall be notified and required promptly to submit two manually signed copies in each language.

Notice of Arbitration

Article 3

No Notice of Arbitration pursuant to Article 3 of the UNCITRAL Rules is to be given.

Representation and Assistance

Article 4

The parties may be represented or assisted by persons of their choice. The names and addresses of such persons must be communicated in writing to the other party; such communication must specify whether the appointment is being made for purposes of representation or assistance.

Notes to Article 4

1. As used in Article 4 the term "parties" means the arbitrating parties.

2. For the purpose of a particular case, the two Governments may each appoint representatives in addition to their Agents and each of the other arbitrating parties may appoint representatives. An appointed representative shall be deemed to be authorized to act before the arbitral tribunal on behalf of the appointing party for all purposes of the case and the acts of the representative shall be binding upon the appointing party. A representative is not required to be licensed to practice law. Parties who appoint a representative shall file with the Registrar notice of appointment in such form as the Registrar may require.

3. Arbitrating parties may also be assisted in proceedings before the arbitral tribunal by one or more persons of their choice. Persons chosen to assist who are not also appointed as representatives are not deemed to be authorized to act before the arbitral tribunal on behalf of the appointing party, to bind the appointing party or to receive notices, communications or documents on behalf of the appointing party. Any such assistant is not required to be licensed to practice law.

SECTION II. COMPOSITION OF THE ARBITRAL TRIBUNAL

Number of Members

Article 5

The composition of Chambers, the assignment of cases to various Chambers, the transfer of cases among Chambers and the relinquishment by Chambers of certain cases to the Full Tribunal will be provided for in orders issued by the President pursuant to his powers under Article III, paragraph 1 of the Claims Settlement Declaration.

Appointment of Members – Articles 6-8

Article 6

1. If a sole arbitrator is to be appointed, either party may propose to the other:

(a) The names of one or more persons, one of whom would serve as the sole arbitrator; and

(b) If no appointing authority has been agreed upon by the parties, the name or names of one or more institutions or persons, one of whom would serve as appointing authority.

2. If within thirty days after receipt by a party of a proposal made in accordance with paragraph 1 the parties have not reached agreement on the choice of a sole arbitrator, the sole arbitrator shall be appointed by the appointing authority agreed upon by the parties. If no appointing authority has been agreed upon by the parties, or if the appointing authority agreed upon refuses to act or fails to appoint the arbitrator within sixty days of the receipt of a party's request therefor, either party may request

the Secretary-General of the Permanent Court of Arbitration at The Hague to designate an appointing authority.

3. The appointing authority shall, at the request of one of the parties, appoint the sole arbitrator as promptly as possible. In making the appointment the appointing authority shall use the following list-procedure, unless both parties agree that the list-procedure should not be used or unless the appointing authority determines in its discretion that the use of the list-procedure is not appropriate for the case:

(a) At the request of one of the parties the appointing authority shall communicate to both parties an identical list containing at least three names;

(b) Within fifteen days after the receipt of this list, each party may return the list to the appointing authority after having deleted the name or names to which he objects and numbered the remaining names on the list in the order of his preference;

(c) After the expiration of the above period of time the appointing authority shall appoint the sole arbitrator from among the names approved on the lists returned to it and in accordance with the order of preference indicated by the parties;

(d) If for any reason the appointment cannot be made according to this procedure, the appointing authority may exercise its discretion in appointing the sole arbitrator.

4. In making the appointment, the appointing authority shall have regard to such considerations as are likely to secure the appointment of an independent and impartial arbitrator and shall take into account as well the advisability of appointing an arbitrator of a nationality other than the nationalities of the parties.

Article 7

1. If three arbitrators are to be appointed, each party shall appoint one arbitrator. The two arbitrators thus appointed shall choose the third arbitrator who will act as the presiding arbitrator of the tribunal.

2. If within thirty days after the receipt of a party's notification of the appointment of an arbitrator the other party has not notified the first party of the arbitrator he has appointed:

(a) The first party may request the appointing authority previously designated by the parties to appoint the second arbitrator; or

(b) If no such authority has been previously designated by the parties, or if the appointing authority previously designated refuses to act or fails to appoint the arbitrator within thirty days after receipt of a party's request therefor, the first party may request the Secretary-General of the Permanent Court of Arbitration at The Hague to designate the appointing authority. The first party may then request the appointing authority so designated to appoint the second arbitrator. In either case, the appointing authority may exercise its discretion in appointing the arbitrator.

3. If within thirty days after the appointment of the second arbitrator the two arbitrators have not agreed on the choice of the presiding arbitrator, the presiding arbitrator shall be appointed by an appointing authority in the same way as a sole arbitrator would be appointed under Article 6.

Article 8

1. When an appointing authority is requested to appoint an arbitrator pursuant to Article 6 or Article 7, the party which makes the request shall send to the appointing authority a copy of the notice of arbitration, a copy of the contract out of or in relation to which the dispute has arisen and a copy of the arbitration agreement if it is not contained in the contract. The appointing authority may require from either party such information as it deems necessary to fulfil its function.

2. Where the names of one or more persons are proposed for appointment as arbitrators, their full names, addresses and nationalities shall be indicated, together with a description of their qualifications.

Note to Articles 6-8

As used in Articles 6, 7 and 8 of the Tribunal Rules, the terms "party" and "parties" refer to the one or both of the two Governments, as the case may be.

Challenge of Members – Articles 9-12

Article 9

A prospective arbitrator shall disclose to those who approach him in connexion with his possible appointment any circumstances likely to give rise to justifiable doubts as to his impartiality or independence. An arbitrator, once appointed or chosen, shall disclose such circumstances to the parties unless they have already been informed by him of these circumstances. When any member of the arbitral tribunal obtains knowledge that any particular case before the arbitral tribunal involves circumstances likely to give rise to justifiable doubts as to his impartiality or independence with respect to that case, he shall disclose such circumstances to the President and, if the President so determines, to the arbitrating parties in the case and, if appropriate, shall disqualify himself as to that case.

Article 10

1. Any arbitrator may be challenged if circumstances exist that give rise to justifiable doubts as to the arbitrator's impartiality or independence.

2. A party may challenge the arbitrator appointed by him only for reasons of which he becomes aware after the appointment has been made.

Article 11

1. A party who intends to challenge an arbitrator shall send notice of his challenge within fifteen days after the appointment of the challenged arbitrator has been notified to the challenging party or within fifteen days after the circumstances mentioned in Articles 9 and 10 became known to that party.

2. The challenge shall be notified to the other party, to the arbitrator who is challenged and to the other members of the arbitral tribunal. The notification shall be in writing and shall state the reasons for the challenge.

3. When an arbitrator has been challenged by one party, the other party may agree to the challenge. The arbitrator may also, after the challenge, withdraw from his office. In neither case does this imply acceptance of the validity of the grounds for the challenge. In both cases the procedure provided in Article 6 or 7 shall be used in full for the appointment of the substitute arbitrator, even if during the process of appointing the challenged arbitrator a party had failed to exercise his right to appoint or to participate in the appointment.

Article 12

1. If the other party does not agree to the challenge and the challenged arbitrator does not withdraw, the decision on the challenge will be made:

(a) When the initial appointment was made by an appointing authority, by that authority;

(b) When the initial appointment was not made by an appointing authority, but an appointing authority has been previously designated, by that authority;

(c) In all other cases, by the appointing authority to be designated in accordance with the procedure for designating an appointing authority as provided for in Article 6.

2. If the appointing authority sustains the challenge, a substitute arbitrator shall be appointed or chosen pursuant to the procedure applicable to the appointment or choice of an arbitrator as provided in Articles 6 to 9 except that, when this procedure would call for the designation of an appointing authority, the appointment of the arbitrator shall be made by the appointing authority which decided on the challenge.

Notes to Articles 9-12

1. As used in Articles 9, 10, 11 and 12 of the Tribunal Rules, with respect to the initial appointment of a member the terms "party" and "parties" mean one or both of the two Governments, as the case may be. After the initial appointment, the terms "party" and "parties" mean the arbitrating party or parties, as the case may be. Arbitrating parties may challenge a member only on the basis of the existence of circumstances which give rise to justifiable doubts as to the member's impartiality or independence with respect to the particular case involved, and not upon any general grounds which may also relate to other cases. Challenges on such general grounds may only be made by one of the two Governments.

2. In applying paragraph 1 of Article 11 of the Tribunal Rules, the period for making a challenge to a member of a Chamber to which a case has been assigned shall be fifteen days after the challenging party is given notice of the the circumstances mentioned in Articles 9 and 10 of the Tribunal Rules became known to that party. In the event the case is relinquished by the Chamber to the Full Tribunal, the period for challenging a member who is not a member of the relinquishing Chamber shall be fifteen days after the challenging party is given notice of the relinguishment, or after the circumstances mentioned in Articles 9 and 10 of the Tribunal Rules became known to that party.

3. In the event a member withdraws with respect to a particular case or if the challenge is sustained, he shall continue to exercise his functions as a member for all other cases and purposes except in respect of that particular case.

4. In the event that a member of a Chamber is challenged with respect to a particular case and withdraws, or if the challenge is sustained, the President will order the transfer of the case to another Chamber.

5. In the event the Full Tribunal is seised of a particular case and a member is challenged with respect to that case and withdraws, or if the challenge is sustained, a substitute member shall be appointed to the Full Tribunal for the purposes of that case in accordance with the procedure set forth in Article III of the Claims Settlement Declaration as was used in appointing the member being substituted. An appointing authority, if needed, shall be designated as provided in Article 12 of the Tribunal Rules.

6. Disclosure statements filed as to each member shall be made available by the Registrar to each arbitrating party in each case.

Replacement of a Member

Article 13

1. In the event of the death or resignation of an arbitrator during the course of the arbitral proceedings, a substitute arbitrator shall be appointed or chosen pursuant to the procedure provided for in Articles 6 to 9 that was applicable to the appointment or choice of the arbitrator being replaced.

2. In the event that an arbitrator fails to act or in the event of the *de jure* or *de facto* impossibility of his performing his functions, the procedure in respect of the challenge and replacement of an arbitrator as provided in the preceding Articles shall apply. In applying the provisions of this paragraph, if the President, after consultation with the other members of the Full Tribunal, determines that the failure of a member to act or his impossibility to perform his functions is due to a temporary illness or other circumstance expected to be of relatively short duration, the member shall not be replaced but a substitute member shall be appointed for the temporary period in accordance with the same procedures as are described in Note 5 to Articles 9-12.

3. In the event of the temporary absence of the President, the senior other member of the Tribunal not appointed by either of the two Governments shall act as President of the Tribunal and as Chairman at the meetings of the Full Tribunal. Seniority shall be based on the date of appointment, or for members appointed on the same date shall be based on age.

4. A substitute member appointed for a temporary period shall continue to serve with respect to any case in which he has participated in the hearing, notwithstanding the member for whom he is a substitute is again available and may work on other Tribunal cases and matters.

5. After the effective date of a member's resignation he shall continue to serve as a member of the Tribunal with respect to all cases in which he had participated in a hearing on the merits, and for that purpose shall be considered a member of the Tribunal instead of the person who replaces him.

Note to Article 13

Iran may, in advance, appoint up to three persons, to be available to act as a substitute member for a temporary period for a specified member, or members, of the Tribunal appointed by Iran; and the United States may, in advance, appoint up to three persons, to be available to act as a substitute member for a temporary period for a specified member, or members of the Tribunal appointed by the United States. The members of the Tribunal appointed by Iran and the United States may select, in advance, by mutual agreement, a person to act as substitute for a temporary period for any of the remaining one third of the members of the Tribunal.

Repetition of Hearings in the Event of Replacement or Substitutioin of a Member

Article 14

If a member of the Full Tribunal or of a Chamber is replaced or if a substitute is appointed for him, the arbitral tribunal shall determine whether all, any part or none of any previous hearings shall be repeated.

SECTION III. ARBITRAL PROCEEDINGS

General Provisions

Article 15

1. Subject to these Rules, the arbitral tribunal may conduct the arbitration in such manner as it considers appropriate, provided that the parties are treated with equality and that at any stage of the proceedings each party is given a full opportunity of presenting his case.

2. If either party so requests at any stage of the proceedings, the arbitral tribunal shall hold hearings for the presentation of evidence by witnesses, including expert witnesses, or for oral argument. In the absence of such a request, the arbitral tribunal

shall decide whether to hold such hearings or whether the proceedings shall be conducted on the basis of documents and other materials.

3. All documents or information supplied to the arbitral tribunal by one party shall at the same time be communicated by that party to the other party.

Notes to Article 15

1. As used in Article 15, the terms "party" and "parties" mean the arbitrating party or parties, as the case may be.

2. In applying paragraph 2 of Article 15, the arbitral tribunal shall determine without hearing any written requests or objections of the concerned arbitrating parties with respect to procedural matters unless it grants or invites oral argument in special circumstances.

3. In complying with paragraph 3 of Article 15, an arbitrating party shall follow the procedures set forth in Article 2 of the Tribunal Rules.

4. The arbitral tribunal may make an order directing the arbitrating parties to appear for a pre-hearing conference. The pre-hearing conference will normally be held only after the Statement of Defence in the case has been received. The order will state the matters to be considered at the pre-hearing conference.

5. The arbitral tribunal may, having satisfied itself that the statement of one of the two Governments – or, under special circumstances, any other person – who is not an arbitrating party in a particular case is likely to assist the tribunal in carrying out its task, permit such Government or person to assist the tribunal by presenting oral or written statements.

Place of Arbitration

Article 16

1. Unless the parties have agreed upon the place where the arbitration is to be held, such place shall be determined by the arbitral tribunal, having regard to the circumstances of the arbitration.

2. The arbitral tribunal may determine the locale of the arbitration within the country agreed upon by the parties. It may hear witnesses and hold meetings for consultation among its members at any place it deems appropriate, having regard to the circumstances of the arbitration.

3. The arbitral tribunal may meet at any place it deems appropriate for the inspection of goods, other property or documents. The parties shall be given sufficient notice to enable them to be present at such inspection.

4. The award shall be made at the place of arbitration.

Note to Article 16

As used in Article 16, paragraphs 1 and 2 of the Tribunal Rules, the term "parties" means the two Governments. As used in Article 16, paragraph 3 of the Tribunal Rules, the term "parties" means the arbitrating parties.

Language

Article 17

1. Subject to an agreement by the parties, the arbitral tribunal shall, promptly after its appointment, determine the language or languages to be used in the proceedings. This determination shall apply to the statement of claim, the statement of defence, and any further written statements and, if oral hearings take place, to the language or languages to be used in such hearings.

2. The arbitral tribunal may order that any documents annexed to the statement of claim or statement of defence, and any supplementary documents or exhibits submitted in the course of the proceedings, delivered in their original language, shall be accompanied by a translation into the language or languages agreed upon by the parties or determined by the arbitral tribunal.

Notes to Article 17

1. As used in Article 17 of the Tribunal Rules, the term "parties" means the two Governments.

2. In accordance with an agreement of the Agents, English and Persian shall be the two official languages to be used in the arbitration proceedings, and these languages shall be used for all oral hearings, decisions and awards.

3. In accordance with the provisions of Article 17 of the Tribunal Rules, the following documents filed with the Tribunal shall be submitted in both English and Persian, unless otherwise agreed by the arbitrating parties:

   (a) The Statement of Claim and its annexes.

(b) The Statement of Defence, and any counter-claim, including any annexes.

(c) The reply (including any annexes) to any counter-claim.

(d) Any further written statement (e.g. reply, rejoinder, brief), including any annexes, which the arbitral tribunal may require or permit an arbitrating party to present.

(e) Any written request to the arbitral tribunal to take action or any objection thereto.

(f) Any challenge to a member.

4. The arbitral tribunal shall determine in each particular case what other documents, documentary exhibits and written evidence, or what parts thereof, shall be submitted in both English and Persian.

5. Any disputes or difficulties regarding translations shall be resolved by the arbitral tribunal.

Statement of Claim

Article 18

1. A party initiating recourse to arbitration before the Tribunal (the "claimant") shall do so by filing a Statement of Claim. Each Statement of Claim shall contain the following particulars:

(a) A demand that the dispute be referred to arbitration by the Tribunal;

(b) The names, nationalities and last known addresses of the parties;

(c) A reference to the debt, contract (including transactions which are the subject of letters of credit or bank guarantees), expropriations or other measures affecting property rights out of or in relation to which the dispute arises and as to which the Tribunal has jurisdiction pursuant to Article II, paragraphs 1 and 2 of the Claims Settlement Declaration;

(d) The general nature of the claim and an indication of the amount involved, if any;

(e) A statement of the facts supporting the claim;

(f) The points at issue;

(g) The relief or remedy sought;

(h) If the claimant has appointed a lawyer or other person for purposes of representation or assistance in connection with the claim, the name and address of such person and an indication whether the appointment is for purposes of representation or assistance;

(i) The name and address of the person to whom communications should be sent on behalf of the claimant (only one such person shall be entitled to be sent communications).

2. It is advisable that claimants (i) annex to their Statements of Claim such documents as will serve clearly to establish the basis of the claim, and/or (ii) add a reference and summary of relevant portions of such documents, and/or (iii) include in the Statement of Claim quotations of relevant portions of such documents.

3. No priority for the scheduling of hearings or the making of awards shall be based on the date of filing the Statement of Claim.

Notes to Article 18

1. No claims with respect to which the Tribunal has jurisdiction within the framework of the Algiers Declarations and pursuant to paragraphs 1 and 2 of Article II of the Claims Settlement Declaration may be filed before October 20, 1981.

2. All Statements of Claim with respect to matters as to which the Tribunal has jurisdiction pursuant to paragraphs 1 and 2 of Article II of the Claims Settlement Declaration which are filed between October 20, 1981 and November 19, 1981 will be deemed to have been filed simultaneously as of October 20, 1981. All such claims filed between November 20, 1981 and December 19, 1981 will be deemed to have been filed simultaneously as of November 20, 1981. All such claims filed between December 20, 1981 and January 19, 1982 will be deemed to have been filed simultaneously as of December 20, 1981.

Statement of Defence

Article 19

1. Within a period of time to be determined by the arbitral tribunal with respect to each case, which should not exceed 135 days, the respondent shall file its Statement of Defence. However, the arbitral tribunal may extend the time-limits if it concludes that such an extension is justified.

2. The Statement of Defence shall reply to the particulars (e), (f) and (g) and include the information required in (h) and (i) of the Statement of Claim (see Article 18, paragraph 1 of the Tribunal Rules). It is advisable that respondents (i) annex to their Statement of Defence such documents as will clearly serve to establish the basis of the defence, and/or (ii) add a reference and summary of the relevant portions of such documents, and/or (iii) include in the Statement of Defence quotations of relevant portions of such documents.

3. In the Statement of Defence, or at a later stage in the arbitral proceedings if the arbitral tribunal decides that the delay was justified under the circumstances, the respondent may make a counter-claim or rely on a claim for the purpose of a set-off, if such counter-claim or set-off is allowed under the Claims Settlement Declaration.

4. The provisions of Article 18, paragraph 1 shall apply to a counter-claim or claim relied on for purpose of a set-off.

Notes to Article 19

1. In determining and extending periods of time pursuant to this Article, the arbitral tribunal will take into account

   (i) the complexity of the case,

   (ii) any special circumstances, including demonstrated hardship to a claimant or respondent, and

   (iii) such other circumstances as it considers appropriate.

   In the event that the arbitral tribunal determines that a requirement to file a large number of Statements of Defence in any particular period would impose an unfair burden on a respondent to a claim or counter-claim, it will in some cases extend the time periods based on the above-mentioned factors or by lot.

2. In the event of a counter-claim or claim relied on for the purpose of a set-off, the claimant against whom it is made will be given the right of reply, and the provisions of paragraph 2 of Article 19 of the Tribunal Rules shall apply.

Amendments to the Claim or Defence

Article 20

During the course of the arbitral proceedings either party may amend or supplement his claim or defence unless the arbitral tribunal considers it inappropriate to allow such amendment having regard to the delay in making it or prejudice to the other party or any other circumstances. However, a claim may not be amended in such a manner that the amended claim falls outside the jurisdiction of the arbitral tribunal.

Note to Article 20

As used in Article 20 of the Tribunal Rules, the term "party" means the arbitrating party.

Pleas as to the Jurisdiction of the Arbitral Tribunal

Article 21

1. The arbitral tribunal shall have the power to rule on objections that it has no jurisdiction, including any objections with respect to the existence or validity of the arbitration clause or of the separate arbitration agreement.

2. The arbitral tribunal shall have the power to determine the existence or the validity of the contract of which an arbitration clause forms a part. For the purpose of article 21, an arbitration clause which forms part of a contract and which provides for arbitration under these Rules shall be treated as an agreement independent of the other terms of the contract. A decision by the arbitral tribunal that the contract is null and void shall not entail *ipso jure* the invalidity of the arbitration clause.

3. A plea that the arbitral tribunal does not have jurisdiction shall be raised not later than in the statement of defence or, with respect to a counter-claim, in the reply to the counter-claim.

4. In general, the arbitral tribunal should rule on a plea concerning its jurisdiction as a preliminary question. However, the arbitral tribunal may proceed with the arbitration and rule on such a plea in their final award.

Further Written Statements

Article 22

The arbitral tribunal shall decide which further written statements, in addition to the statement of claim and the statement of defence, shall be required from the parties or may be presented by them and shall fix the periods of time for communicating such statements.

Note to Article 22

As used in Article 22 of the Tribunal Rules, the term "parties" means the arbitrating parties.

Periods of Time

Article 23

The periods of time fixed by the arbitral tribunal for the communication of written statements (excluding the Statement of Defence) should not exceed 90 days. However, the arbitral tribunal may extend the time-limits if it concludes that an extension is justified.

Evidence and Hearings – Articles 24-25

Article 24

1. Each party shall have the burden of proving the facts relied on to support his claim or defence.

2. The arbitral tribunal may, if it considers it appropriate, require a party to deliver to the tribunal and to the other party, within such a period of time as the arbitral tribunal shall decide, a summary of the documents and other evidence which that party intends to present in support of the facts in issue set out in his statement of claim or statement of defence.

3. At any time during the arbitral proceedings the arbitral tribunal may require the parties to produce documents, exhibits or other evidence within such a period of time as the tribunal shall determine.

Note to Article 24

As used in Article 24 of the Tribunal Rules, the terms "party" and "parties" mean the arbitrating party or parties, as the case may be.

Article 25

1. In the event of an oral hearing, the arbitral tribunal shall give the parties adequate advance notice of the date, time and place thereof.

2. If witnesses are to be heard, at least *thirty* days before the hearing each party shall communicate to the arbitral tribunal and to the other party the names and addresses of the witnesses he intends to present, the subject upon and the languages in which such witnesses will give their testimony.

3. The arbitral tribunal shall make arrangements for the translation of oral statements made at a hearing and for a record of the hearing if either is deemed necessary by the tribunal under the circumstances of the case, or if the parties have agreed thereto and have communicated such agreement to the tribunal at least fifteen days before the hearing.

4. Hearings shall be held *in camera* unless the parties agree otherwise. The arbitral tribunal may require the retirement of any witness or witnesses during the testimony of other witnesses. The arbitral tribunal is free to determine the manner in which witnesses are examined.

5. Evidence of witnesses may also be presented in the form of written statements signed by them.

6. The arbitral tribunal shall determine the admissibility, relevance, materiality and weight of the evidence offered.

Notes to Article 25

1. As used in Article 25 of the Tribunal Rules, the terms "party" and "parties" mean the arbitrating party or parties, as the case may be, except that, as used in paragraph 4 of Article 25, the term "parties" means the two Governments and the arbitrating parties.

2. The information concerning witnesses which an arbitrating party must communicate pursuant to paragraph 2 of Article 25 of the Tribunal Rules is not required with respect to any witnesses which an arbitrating party may later decide to present to rebut evidence presented by the other arbitrating party. However, such information concerning any rebuttal witness shall be communicated to the arbitral tribunal and the other arbitrating parties as far in advance of hearing the witness as is reasonably possible.

3. With respect to paragraph 3 of Article 25 of the Tribunal Rules, the Secretary-General shall make arrangements for a tape-recording or stenographic record of hearings or parts of hearings if the arbitral tribunal so determines. If the arbitral tribunal determines that a transcript shall be made of any such tape-recording or stenographic record, the arbitrating parties in that case, or their authorized representatives, shall be permitted to read the transcript.

4. Any arbitrating party in the case may make a stenographic record of the hearings, or parts of the hearings, and, in that event, shall make a transcript thereof available to the arbitral tribunal without charge. Arbitrating parties are not permitted to make tape-recordings of hearings or other proceedings.

5. Notwithstanding the provisions of paragraph 4 of Article 25, the arbitral tribunal may at its discretion permit representatives of arbitrating parties in other cases which present similar issues of fact or law to be present to observe all or part of the hearing in a particular case, subject to the prior approval of the arbitrating parties in the particular case. The Agents of the two Governments are permitted to be present at pre-hearing conferences and hearings.

6. In applying paragraph 4 of Article 25 of the Tribunal Rules, the following provisions shall determine the manner in which witnesses are examined.

   (a) Before giving any evidence each witness shall make the following declaration: "I solemnly declare upon my honour and conscience that I will speak the truth, the whole truth and nothing but the truth."

   (b) Witnesses may be examined by the presiding member and the other members of the arbitral tribunal. Also, when permitted by the arbitral tribunal, the representatives of the arbitrating parties in the case may ask questions, subject to the control of the presiding member.

7. The Secretary-General shall draft minutes of each hearing. After each member of the arbitral tribunal present at the hearing has been given the opportunity to comment on the draft minutes, the minutes, with any corrections approved by a majority of members who were present, shall be signed by the presiding

member and the Secretary-General. The arbitrating parties in the case, or their representatives, shall be permitted to read such minutes.

Interim Measures of Protection

Article 26

1. At the request of either party, the arbitral tribunal may take any interim measures it deems necessary in respect of the subject-matter of the dispute, including measures for the conservation of the goods forming the subject-matter in dispute, such as ordering their deposit with a third person or the sale of perishable goods.

2. Such interim measures may be established in the form of an interim award. The arbitral tribunal shall be entitled to require security for the costs of such measures.

3. A request for interim measures addressed by any party to a judicial authority shall not be deemed incompatible with the agreement to arbitrate, or as a waiver of that agreement.

Note to Article 26

As used in Article 26 of the Tribunal Rules, the term "party" means the arbitrating party.

Experts

Article 27

1. The arbitral tribunal may appoint one or more experts to report to it, in writing, on specific issues to be determined by the tribunal. A copy of the expert's terms of reference, established by the arbitral tribunal, shall be communicated to the parties.

2. The parties shall give the expert any relevant information or produce for his inspection any relevant documents or goods that he may require of them. Any dispute between a party and such expert as to the relevance of the required information or production shall be referred to the arbitral tribunal for decision. The expert shall invite a representative of each arbitrating party to attend any site inspection, and, when the arbitral tribunal so determines, a representative of each arbitrating party shall be invited to attend other inspections made by the expert.

3. Upon receipt of the expert's report, the arbitral tribunal shall communicate a copy of the report to the parties who shall be given the opportunity to express, in writing, their opinion on the report. A party shall be entitled to examine any document on which the expert has relied in his report.

4. At the request of either party the expert, after delivery of the report, may be heard at a hearing where the parties shall have the opportunity to be present and to interrogate the expert. At this hearing either party may present expert witnesses in order to testify on the points at issue. The provisions of Article 25 shall be applicable to such proceedings.

Notes to Article 27

1. As used in Article 27 of the Tribunal Rules, the terms "party" and "parties" mean the arbitrating party or parties, as the case may be.
2. Every expert, before beginning the performance of his duties, shall make the following declaration: "I solemnly declare upon my honour and conscience that I will perform my duties in accordance with my sincere belief and will keep confidential all matters relating to the performance of my task."

Default

Article 28

1. If, within the period of time fixed by the arbitral tribunal, the claimant has failed to communicate his claim without showing sufficient cause for such failure, the arbitral tribunal shall issue an order for the termination of the arbitral proceedings. If, within the period of time fixed by the arbitral tribunal, the respondent has failed to communicate his statement of defence without showing sufficient cause for such failure, the arbitral tribunal shall order that the proceedings continue.

2. If one of the parties, duly notified under these Rules, fails to appear at a hearing, without showing sufficient cause for such failure, the arbitral tribunal may proceed with the arbitration.

3. If one of the parties, duly invited to produce documentary evidence, fails to do so within the established period of time, without showing sufficient cause for such failure, the arbitral tribunal may make the award on the evidence before it.

Note to Article 28

As used in Article 28 of the Tribunal Rules, the term "parties" means the arbitrating parties.

Closure of Hearings

Article 29

1. The arbitral tribunal may inquire of the parties if they have any further proof to offer or witnesses to be heard or submissions to make and, if there are none, it may declare the hearings closed.

2. The arbitral tribunal may, if it considers it necessary owing to exceptional circumstances, decide, on its own motion or upon application of a party, to reopen the hearings at any time before the award is made.

Note to Article 29

As used in Article 29 of the Tribunal Rules, the terms "party" and "parties" mean the arbitrating party or parties, as the case may be.

Waiver of Rules

Article 30

A party who knows that any provision of, or requirement under, these Rules has not been complied with and yet proceeds with the arbitration without promptly stating his objection to such non-compliance, shall be deemed to have waived his right to object.

Note to Article 30

As used in Article 30 of the Tribunal Rules, the term "party" means the arbitrating party.

Decisions

Article 31

1. When there are three arbitrators, any award or other decision of the arbitral tribunal shall be made by a majority of the arbitrators.

2. In the case of questions of procedure, when there is no majority or when the arbitral tribunal so authorizes, the presiding arbitrator may decide on his own, subject to revision, if any, by the arbitral tribunal.

Notes to Article 31

1. Any award or other decision of the arbitral tribunal pursuant to paragraph 1 of Article 31 shall be made by a majority of its members.
2. The arbitral tribunal shall deliberate in private. Its deliberations shall be and remain secret. Only the members of the arbitral tribunal shall take part in the deliberations. The Secretary-General may be present. No other person may be admitted except by special decision of the arbitral tribunal. Any question which is to be voted upon shall be formulated in precise terms in English and Persian and the text shall, if a member so requests, be distributed before the vote is taken. The minutes of the private sittings of the arbitral tribunal shall be secret.

Form and Effect of Award

Article 32

1. In addition to making a final award, the arbitral tribunal shall be entitled to make interim, interlocutory, or partial awards.

2. The award shall be made in writing and shall be final and binding on the parties. The parties undertake to carry out the award without delay.

3. The arbitral tribunal shall state the reasons upon which the award is based, unless the parties have agreed that no reasons are to be given. Any arbitrator may request that his dissenting vote or his dissenting vote and the reasons therefor be recorded.

4. An award shall be signed by the arbitrators and it shall contain the date on which and the place where the award was made. Where there are three arbitrators and one of them fails to sign, the award shall state the reason for the absence of the signature.

5. All awards and other decisions shall be made available to the public, except that upon the request of one or more arbitrating parties, the arbitral tribunal may determine that it will not make the entire award or other decision public, but will make public only portions thereof from which the identity of the parties, other identifying facts and trade or military secrets have been deleted.

6. Copies of the award signed by the arbitrators shall be communicated to the parties by the arbitral tribunal.

7. If the arbitration law of the country where the award is made requires that the award be filed or registered by the arbitral tribunal, the tribunal shall comply with this requirement within the period of time required by law.

Note to Article 32

As used in Article 32 of the Tribunal Rules, the term "parties" means the arbitrating parties.

Applicable Law

Article 33

1. The arbitral tribunal shall decide all cases on the basis of respect for law, applying such choice of law rules and principles of commercial and international law as the arbitral tribunal determines to be applicable, taking into account relevant usages of the trade, contract provisions and changed circumstances.

2. The arbitral tribunal shall decide *ex aequo et bono* only if the arbitrating parties have expressly and in writing authorized it to do so.

Note to Article 33

Paragraph 1 of Article 33 corresponds to Article V of the Claims Settlement Declaration.

Settlement or Other Grounds for Termination

Article 34

1. If, before the award is made, the parties agree on a settlement of the dispute, the arbitral tribunal shall either issue an order for the termination of the arbitral pro-

ceedings or, if requested by both parties and accepted by the tribunal, record the settlement in the form of an arbitral award on agreed terms. The arbitral tribunal is not obliged to give reasons for such an award.

2. If, before the award is made, the continuation of the arbitral proceedings becomes unnecessary or impossible for any reason not mentioned in paragraph 1, the arbitral tribunal shall inform the parties of its intention to issue an order for the termination of the proceedings. The arbitral tribunal shall have the power to issue such an order unless a party raises justifiable grounds for objection.

3. Copies of the order for termination of the arbitral proceedings or of the arbitral award on agreed terms, signed by the arbitrators, shall be communicated by the arbitral tribunal to the parties. Where an arbitral award on agreed terms is made, the provisions of Article 32, paragraphs 2 and 4 to 7, shall apply.

Note to Article 34

As used in Article 34 of the Tribunal Rules, the terms "party" and "parties" mean the arbitrating party or parties, as the case may be.

Interpretation of the Award

Article 35

1. Within thirty days after the receipt of the award, either party, with notice to the other party, may request that the arbitral tribunal give an interpretation of the award.

2. The interpretation shall be given in writing within forty-five days after the receipt of the request. The interpretation shall form part of the award and the provisions of Article 32, paragraphs 2 to 7, shall apply.

Note to Article 35

As used in Article 35 of the Tribunal Rules, the term "party" means the arbitrating party.

Correction of the Award

Article 36

1. Within thirty days after the receipt of the award, either party, with notice to the other party, may request the arbitral tribunal to correct in the award any errors in computation, any clerical or typographical errors, or any errors of similar nature. The arbitral tribunal may within thirty days after the communication of the award make such corrections on its own initiative.

2. Such corrections shall be in writing, and the provisions of Article 32, paragraphs 2 to 7, shall apply.

Note to Article 36

As used in Article 36 of the Tribunal Rules, the term "party" means the arbitrating party.

Additional Award

Article 37

1. Within thirty days after the receipt of the award, either party, with notice to the other party, may request the arbitral tribunal to make an additional award as to claims presented in the arbitral proceedings but omitted from the award.

2. If the arbitral tribunal considers the request for an additional award to be justified and considers that the omission can be rectified without any further hearings or evidence, it shall complete its award within sixty days after the receipt of the request.

3. When an additional award is made, the provisions of Article 32, paragraphs 2 to 7, shall apply.

Note to Article 37

As used in Article 37 of the Tribunal Rules, the term "party" means the arbitrating party.

Costs – Articles 38-40

Article 38

1. The arbitral tribunal shall fix the costs of arbitration in its award. The term "costs" includes only:

(a) The costs of expert advice and of other special assistance required for a particular case by the arbitral tribunal;

(b) The travel and other expenses of witnesses to the extent such expenses are approved by the arbitral tribunal;

(c) The costs for legal representation and assistance of the successful party if such costs were claimed during the arbitral proceedings, and only to the extent that the arbitral tribunal determines that the amount of such costs is reasonable.

2. The Full Tribunal shall fix the fees and expenses of the Tribunal which, in accordance with Article VI, paragraph 3 of the Claims Settlement Declaration, shall be borne equally by the two Governments.

Note to Article 38

As used in Article 38 of the Tribunal Rules, the term "party" means the arbitrating party.

Article 39

1. The fees of the arbitral tribunal shall be reasonable in amount, taking into account the amount in dispute, the complexity of the subject-matter, the time spent by the arbitrators and any other relevant circumstances of the case.

2. If an appointing authority has been agreed upon by the parties or designated by the Secretary-General of the Permanent Court of Arbitration at The Hague, and if that authority has issued a schedule of fees for arbitrators in international cases which it administers, the arbitral tribunal in fixing its fees shall take that schedule of fees into account to the extent that it considers appropriate in the circumstances of the case.

3. If such appointing authority has not issued a schedule of fees for arbitration in international cases, any party may at any time request the appointing authority to furnish a statement setting forth the basis for establishing fees which is customarily

followed in international cases in which the authority appoints arbitrators. If the appointing authority consents to provide such a statement, the arbitral tribunal in fixing its fees shall take such information into account to the extent that it considers appropriate in the circumstances of the case.

4. In cases referred to in paragraphs 2 and 3, when a party so requests and the appointing authority consents to perform the function, the arbitral tribunal shall fix its fees only after consultation with the appointing authority which may make any comment it deems appropriate to the arbitral tribunal concerning the fees.

Note to Article 39

As used in Article 39 of the Tribunal Rules, the terms "party" and "parties" mean one or both of the two Governments, as the case may be.

Article 40

1. Except as provided in paragraph 2, the costs of arbitration referred to in paragraphs 1(a) and 1(b) of Article 38 shall in principle be borne by the unsuccessful party. However, the arbitral tribunal may apportion each of such costs between the parties if it determines that apportionment is reasonable, taking into account the circumstances of the case.

2. With respect to the costs of legal representation and assistance referred to in Article 38, paragraph 1(c), the arbitral tribunal, taking into account the circumstances of the case, shall be free to determine which party shall bear such costs or may apportion such costs between the parties if it determines that apportionment is reasonable.

3. When the arbitral tribunal issues an order for the termination of the arbitral proceedings it shall fix the costs of arbitration referred to in Article 38 in the text of that order.

4. No additional fees may be charged by an arbitral tribunal for interpretation or correction or completion of its award under Articles 35 to 37.

Note to Article 40

As used in Article 40 of the Tribunal Rules, the terms "party" and "parties" mean the arbitrating party or parties, as the case may be.

Deposit of Costs

Article 41

1. During the course of its proceedings the Full Tribunal may from time to time determine the costs referred to in paragraph 2 of Article 38 and may request each of the two Governments to deposit equal amounts as advances for such costs.

2. The arbitral may request each arbitrating party to deposit an amount determined by it as advances for the costs referred to in paragraph 1(a) of Article 38.

3. If the required deposits are not paid in full within the time fixed by the arbitral tribunal, the arbitral tribunal shall so inform the parties in order that one or another of them may make the required payment. If such payment is not made, the arbitral tribunal may order the suspension or termination of the arbitral proceedings or may take such action to permit continuation of the proceedings as is appropriate under the circumstances of the case.

4. The Secretary-General shall transmit monthly, quarterly and annual financial statements to the Full Tribunal and to the Agents. The accounts of the Tribunal shall be audited annually by an independent qualified accountant approved by the Full Tribunal. The Secretary-General shall transmit copies of the audit report to the Full Tribunal and to the Agents. At the request of either Agent, the annual audit shall be reviewed by an Audit Committee composed of three professionally qualified persons, one appointed by each Agent and one by the President. The Audit Committee shall submit its report to the Full Tribunal, to the Agents, and to the Secretary-General.

5. After the termination of the work of the Tribunal, it shall, after a final audit render an accounting to the two Governments of the deposits received and return any unexpended balance to the two Governments.

Note to Article 41

As used in paragraph 3, insofar as it refers to deposits made pursuant to paragraph 1 of Article 41 of the Tribunal Rules, the term "parties" means the two Governments; insofar as it refers to deposits made pursuant to paragraph 2 that term means the arbitrating parties.

ANNEX II

RESOLUTION 687 (1991)

Adopted by the Security Council at its 2981st meeting, on 3 April 1991

The Security Council,

Recalling its resolutions 660 (1990) of 2 August 1990, 661 (1990) of 6 August 1990, 662 (1990) of 9 August 1990, 664 (1990) of 18 August 1990, 665 (1990) of 25 August 1990, 666 (1990) of 13 September 1990, 667 (1990) of 16 September 1990, 669 (1990) of 24 September 1990, 670 (1990) of 25 September 1990, 674 (1990) of 29 October 1990, 677 (1990) of 28 November 1990, 678 (1990) of 29 November 1990 and 686 (1991) of 2 March 1991,

Welcoming the restoration to Kuwait of its sovereignty, independence and territorial integrity and the return of its legitimate Government,

Affirming the commitment of all Member States to the sovereignty, territorial integrity and political independence of Kuwait and Iraq, and noting the intention expressed by the Member States cooperating with Kuwait under paragraph 2 of resolution 678 (1990) to bring their military presence in Iraq to an end as soon as possible consistent with paragraph 8 of resolution 686 (1991),

Reaffirming the need to be assured of Iraq's peaceful intentions in the light of its unlawful invasion and occupation of Kuwait,

Taking note of the letter sent by the Minister for Foreign Affairs of Iraq on 27 February 1991 and those sent pursuant to resolution 686 (1991),

Noting that Iraq and Kuwait, as independent sovereign States, signed at Baghdad on 4 October 1963 "Agreed Minutes Between the State of Kuwait and the Republic of Iraq Regarding the Restoration of Friendly Relations, Recognition and Related Matters", thereby recognizing formally the boundary between Iraq and Kuwait and the allocation of islands, which were registered with the United Nations in accordance with Article 102 of the Charter of the United Nations and in which Iraq recognized the independence and complete sovereignty of the State of Kuwait within its borders as specified and accepted in the letter of the Prime Minister of Iraq dated 21

July 1932, and as accepted by the Ruler of Kuwait in his letter dated 10 August 1932,

Conscious of the need for demarcation of the said boundary,

Conscious also of the statements by Iraq threatening to use weapons in violation of its obligations under the Geneva Protocol for the Prohibition of the Use in War of Asphyxiating, Poisonous or Other Gases, and of Bacteriological Methods of Warfare, signed at Geneva on 17 June 1925, and of its prior use of chemical weapons and affirming that grave consequences would follow any further use by Iraq of such weapons,

Recalling that Iraq has subscribed to the Declaration adopted by all States participating in the Conference of States Parties to the 1925 Geneva Protocol and Other Interested States, held in Paris from 7 to 11 January 1989, establishing the objective of universal elimination of chemical and biological weapons,

Recalling also that Iraq has signed the Convention on the Prohibition of the Development, Production and Stockpiling of Bacteriological (Biological) and Toxin Weapons and on Their Destruction, of 10 April 1972,

Noting the importance of Iraq ratifying this Convention,

Noting moreover the importance of all States adhering to this Convention and encouraging its forthcoming Review Conference to reinforce the authority, efficiency and universal scope of the convention,

Stressing the importance of an early conclusion by the Conference on Disarmament of its work on a Convention on the Universal Prohibition of Chemical Weapons and of universal adherence thereto,

Aware of the use by Iraq of ballistic missiles in unprovoked attacks and therefore of the need to take specific measures in regard to such missiles located in Iraq,

Concerned by the reports in the hands of Member States that Iraq has attempted to acquire materials for a nuclear-weapons programme contrary to its obligations under the Treaty on the Non-Proliferation of Nuclear Weapons of 1 July 1968,

Recalling the objective of the establishment of a nuclear-weapons-free zone in the region of the Middle East,

Conscious of the threat that all weapons of mass destruction pose to peace and security in the area and of the need to work towards the establishment in the Middle East of a zone free of such weapons,

Conscious also of the objective of achieving balanced and comprehensive control of armaments in the region,

Conscious further of the importance of achieving the objectives noted above using all available means, including a dialogue among the States of the region,

Noting that resolution 686 (1991) marked the lifting of the measures imposed by resolution 661 (1990) in so far as they applied to Kuwait,

Noting that despite the progress being made in fulfilling the obligations of resolution 686 (1991), many Kuwaiti and third country nationals are still not accounted for and property remains unreturned,

Recalling the International Convention against the Taking of Hostages, opened for signature at New York on 18 December 1979, which categorizes all acts of taking hostages as manifestations of international terrorism,

Deploring threats made by Iraq during the recent conflict to make use of terrorism against targets outside Iraq and the taking of hostages by Iraq,

Taking note with grave concern of the reports of the Secretary-General of 20 March 1991 and 28 March 1991, and conscious of the necessity to meet urgently the humanitarian needs in Kuwait and Iraq,

Bearing in mind its objective of restoring international peace and security in the area as set out in recent resolutions of the Security Council,

Conscious of the need to take the following measures acting under Chapter VII of the Charter,

1. Affirms all thirteen resolutions noted above, except as expressly changed below to achieve the goals of this resolution, including a formal cease-fire;

A

2. Demands that Iraq and Kuwait respect the inviolability of the international boundary and the allocation of islands set out in the "Agreed Minutes Between the State of Kuwait and the Republic of Iraq Regarding the Restoration of Friendly

Relations, Recognition and Related Matters", signed by them in the exercise of their sovereignty at Baghdad on 4 October 1963 and registered with the United Nations and published by the United Nations in document 7063, United Nations, Treaty Series, 1964;

3. Calls upon the Secretary-General to lend his assistance to make arrangements with Iraq and Kuwait to demarcate the boundary between Iraq and Kuwait, drawing on appropriate material, including the map transmitted by Security Council document S/22412 and to report back to the Security Council within one month;

4. Decides to guarantee the inviolability of the above-mentioned international boundary and to take as appropriate all necessary measures to that end in accordance with the Charter of the United Nations;

B

5. Requests the Secretary-General, after consulting with Iraq and Kuwait, to submit within three days to the Security Council for its approval a plan for the immediate deployment of a United Nations observer unit to monitor the Khor Abdullah and a demilitarized zone, which is hereby established, extending ten kilometres into Iraq and five kilometres into Kuwait from the boundary referred to in the "Agreed Minutes Between the State of Kuwait and the Republic of Iraq Regarding the Restoration of Friendly Relations, Recognition and Related Matters" of 4 October 1963; to deter violations of the boundary through its presence in and surveillance of the demilitarized zone; to observe any hostile or potentially hostile action mounted from the territory of one State to the other; and for the Secretary-General to report regularly to the Security Council on the operations of the unit, and immediately if there are serious violations of the zone or potential threats to peace;

6. Notes that as soon as the Secretary-General notifies the Security Council of the completion of the deployment of the United Nations observer unit, the conditions will be established for the Member States cooperating with Kuwait in accordance with resolution 678 (1990) to bring their military presence in Iraq to an end consistent with resolution 686 (1991);

C

7. Invites Iraq to reaffirm unconditionally its obligations under the Geneva Protocol for the Prohibition of the Use in War of Asphyxiating, Poisonous or Other Gases, and of Bacteriological Methods of Warfare, signed at Geneva on 17 June 1925, and to ratify the Convention on the Prohibition of the Development, Production and

Stockpiling of Bacteriological (Biological) and Toxin Weapons and on Their Destruction, of 10 April 1972;

8. Decides that Iraq shall unconditionally accept the destruction, removal, or rendering harmless, under international supervision, of:

(a) All chemical and biological weapons and all stocks of agents and all related subsystems and components and all research, development, support and manufacturing facilities;

(b) All ballistic missiles with a range greater than 150 kilometres and related major parts, and repair and production facilities;

9. Decides, for the implementation of paragraph 8 above, the following:

(a) Iraq shall submit to the Secretary-General, within fifteen days of the adoption of the present resolution, a declaration of the locations, amounts and types of all items specified in paragraph 8 and agree to urgent, on-site inspection as specified below;

(b) The Secretary-General, in consultation with the appropriate Governments and, where appropriate, with the Director-General of the World Health Organization, within forty-five days of the passage of the present resolution, shall develop, and submit to the Council for approval, a plan calling for the completion of the following acts within forty-five days of such approval:

(i) The forming of a Special Commission, which shall carry out immediate on-site inspection of Iraq's biological, chemical and missile capabilities, based on Iraq's declarations and the designation of any additional locations by the Special Commission itself;

(ii) The yielding by Iraq of possession to the Special Commission for destruction, removal or rendering harmless, taking into account the requirements of public safety, of all items specified under paragraph 8(a) above, including items at the additional locations designated by the Special Commission under paragraph 9(b)(i) above and the destruction by Iraq, under the supervision of the Special Commission, of all its missile capabilities, including launchers, as specified under paragraph 8(b) above;

(iii) The provision by the Special Commission of the assistance and cooperation to the Director-General of the International Atomic Energy Agency required in paragraphs 12 and 13 below;

10. Decides that Iraq shall unconditionally undertake not to use, develop, construct or acquire any of the items specified in paragraphs 8 and 9 above and requests the Secretary-General, in consultation with the Special Commission, to develop a plan for the future ongoing monitoring and verification of Iraq's compliance with this paragraph, to be submitted to the Security Council for approval within one hundred and twenty days of the passage of this resolution;

11. Invites Iraq to reaffirm unconditionally its obligations under the Treaty on the Non-Proliferation of Nuclear Weapons of 1 July 1968;

12. Decides that Iraq shall unconditionally agree not to acquire or develop nuclear weapons or nuclear-weapons-usable material or any subsystems or components or any research, development, support or manufacturing facilities related to the above; to submit to the Secretary-General and the Director-General of the International Atomic Energy Agency within fifteen days of the adoption of the present resolution a declaration of the locations, amounts, and types of all items specified above; to place all of its nuclear-weapons-usable materials under the exclusive control, for custody and removal, of the International Atomic Energy Agency, with the assistance and cooperation of the Special Commission as provided for in the plan of the Secretary-General discussed in paragraph 9(b) above; to accept, in accordance with the arrangements provided for in paragraph 13 below, urgent on-site inspection and the destruction, removal or rendering harmless as appropriate of all items specified above; and to accept the plan discussed in paragraph 13 below for the future ongoing monitoring and verification of its compliance with these undertakings;

13. Requests the Director-General of the International Atomic Energy Agency, through the Secretary-General, with the assistance and cooperation of the Special Commission as provided for in the plan of the Secretary-General in paragraph 9(b) above, to carry out immediate on-site inspection of Iraq's nuclear capabilities based on Iraq's declarations and the designation of any additional locations by the Special Commission; to develop a plan for submission to the Security Council within forty-five days calling for the destruction, removal, or rendering harmless as appropriate of all items listed in paragraph 12 above; to carry out the plan within forty-five days following approval by the Security Council; and to develop a plan, taking into account the rights and obligations of Iraq under the Treaty on the Non-Proliferation of Nuclear Weapons of 1 July 1968, for the future ongoing monitoring and verification of Iraq's compliance with paragraph 12 above, including an inventory of all nuclear material in Iraq subject to the Agency's verification and inspections to confirm that Agency safeguards cover all relevant nuclear activities in Iraq, to be submitted to the Security Council for approval within one hundred and twenty days of the passage of the present resolution;

14. Takes note that the actions to be taken by Iraq in paragraphs 8, 9, 10, 11, 12 and 13 of the present resolution represent steps towards the goal of establishing in the Middle East a zone free from weapons of mass destruction and all missiles for their delivery and the objective of a global ban on chemical weapons;

D

15. Requests the Secretary-General to report to the Security Council on the steps taken to facilitate the return of all Kuwaiti property seized by Iraq, including a list of any property that Kuwait claims has not been returned or which has not been returned intact;

E

16. Reaffirms that Iraq, without prejudice to the debts and obligations of Iraq arising prior to 2 August 1990, which will be addressed through the normal mechanisms, is liable under international law for any direct loss, damage, including environmental damage and the depletion of natural resources, or injury to foreign Governments, nationals and corporations, as a result of Iraq's unlawful invasion and occupation of Kuwait;

17. Decides that all Iraqi statements made since 2 August 1990 repudiating its foreign debt are null and void, and demands that Iraq adhere scrupulously to all of its obligations concerning servicing and repayment of its foreign debt;

18. Decides also to create a fund to pay compensation for claims that fall within paragraph 16 above and to establish a Commission that will administer the fund;

19. Directs the Secretary-General to develop and present to the Security Council for decision, no later than thirty days following the adoption of the present resolution, recommendations for the fund to meet the requirement for the payment of claims established in accordance with paragraph 18 above and for a programme to implement the decisions in paragraphs 16, 17 and 18 above, including: administration of the fund; mechanisms for determining the appropriate level of Iraq's contribution to the fund based on a percentage of the value of the exports of petroleum and petroleum products from Iraq not to exceed a figure to be suggested to the Council by the Secretary-General, taking into account the requirements of the people of Iraq, Iraq's payment capacity as assessed in conjunction with the international financial institutions taking into consideration external debt service, and the needs of the Iraqi economy; arrangements for ensuring that payments are made to the fund; the process by which funds will be allocated and claims paid; appropriate procedures for eval-

uating losses, listing claims and verifying their validity and resolving disputed claims in respect of Iraq's liability as specified in paragraph 16 above; and the composition of the Commission designated above;

F

20. Decides, effective immediately, that the prohibitions against the sale or supply to Iraq of commodities or products, other than medicine and health supplies, and prohibitions against financial transactions related thereto contained in resolution 661 (1990) shall not apply to foodstuffs notified to the Security Council Committee established by resolution 661 (1990) concerning the situation between Iraq and Kuwait or, with the approval of that Committee, under the simplified and accelerated "no-objection" procedure, to materials and supplies for essential civilian needs as identified in the report of the Secretary-General dated 20 March 1991, and in any further findings of humanitarian need by the Committee;

21. Decides that the Security Council shall review the provisions of paragraph 20 above every sixty days in the light of the policies and practices of the Government of Iraq, including the implementation of all relevant resolutions of the Security Council, for the purpose of determining whether to reduce or lift the prohibitions referred to therein;

22. Decides that upon the approval by the Security Council of the programme called for in paragraph 19 above and upon Council agreement that Iraq has completed all actions contemplated in paragraphs 8, 9, 10, 11, 12 and 13 above, the prohibitions against the import of commodities and products originating in Iraq and the prohibitions against financial transactions related thereto contained in resolution 661 (1990) shall have no further force or effect;

23. Decides that, pending action by the Security Council under paragraph 22 above, the Security Council Committee established by resolution 661 (1990) shall be empowered to approve, when required to assure adequate financial resources on the part of Iraq to carry out the activities under paragraph 20 above, exceptions to the prohibition against the import of commodities and products originating in Iraq;

24. Decides that, in accordance with resolution 661 (1990) and subsequent related resolutions and until a further decision is taken by the Security Council, all States shall continue to prevent the sale or supply, or the promotion or facilitation of such sale or supply, to Iraq by their nationals, or from their territories or using their flag vessels or aircraft, of:

(a) Arms and related material of all types, specifically including the sale or transfer through other means of all forms of conventional military equipment, including for paramilitary forces, and spare parts and components and their means of production, for such equipment;

(b) Items specified and defined in paragraphs 8 and 12 above not otherwise covered above;

(c) Technology under licensing or other transfer arrangements used in the production, utilization or stockpiling of items specified in subparagraphs (a) and (b) above;

(d) Personnel or materials for training or technical support services relating to the design, development, manufacture, use, maintenance or support of items specified in subparagraphs (a) and (b) above;

25. Calls upon all States and international organizations to act strictly in accordance with paragraph 24 above, notwithstanding the existence of any contracts, agreements, licences or any other arrangements;

26. Requests the Secretary-General, in consultation with appropriate Governments, to develop within sixty days, for the approval of the Security Council, guidelines to facilitate full international implementation of paragraphs 24 and 25 above and paragraph 27 below, and to make them available to all States and to establish a procedure for updating these guidelines periodically;

27. Calls upon all States to maintain such national controls and procedures and to take such other actions consistent with the guidelines to be established by the Security Council under paragraph 26 above as may be necessary to ensure compliance with the terms of paragraph 24 above, and calls upon international organizations to take all appropriate steps to assist in ensuring such full compliance;

28. Agrees to review its decisions in paragraphs 22, 23, 24 and 25 above, except for the items specified and defined in paragraphs 8 and 12 above, on a regular basis and in any case one hundred and twenty days following passage of the present resolution, taking into account Iraq's compliance with the resolution and general progress towards the control of armaments in the region;

29. Decides that all States, including Iraq, shall take the necessary measures to ensure that no claim shall lie at the instance of the Government of Iraq, or of any person or body in Iraq, or of any person claiming through or for the benefit of any such person or body, in connection with any contract or other transaction where its

performance was affected by reason of the measures taken by the Security Council in resolution 661 (1990) and related resolutions;

G

30. Decides that, in furtherance of its commitment to facilitate the repatriation of all Kuwaiti and third country nationals, Iraq shall extend all necessary cooperation to the International Committee of the Red Cross, providing lists of such persons, facilitating the access of the International Committee of the Red Cross to all such persons wherever located or detained and facilitating the search by the International Committee of the Red Cross for those Kuwaiti and third country nationals still unaccounted for;

31. Invites the International Committee of the Red Cross to keep the Secretary-General apprised as appropriate of all activities undertaken in connection with facilitating the repatriation or return of all Kuwaiti and third country nationals or their remains present in Iraq on or after 2 August 1990;

H

32. Requires Iraq to inform the Security Council that it will not commit or support any act of international terrorism or allow any organization directed towards commission of such acts to operate within its territory and to condemn unequivocally and renounce all acts, methods and practices of terrorism;

I

33. Declares that, upon official notification by Iraq to the Secretary-General and to the Security Council of its acceptance of the provisions above, a formal cease-fire is effective between Iraq and Kuwait and the Member States cooperating with Kuwait in accordance with resolution 678 (1990);

34. Decides to remain seized of the matter and to take such further steps as may be required for the implementation of the present resolution and to secure peace and security in the area.

Decisions Taken by the Governing Council of the United Nations Compensation Commission

UNITED
NATIONS

S

Security Council

Distr.
GENERAL

S/AC.26/1991/1
2 August 1991

Original: ENGLISH

FIRST SESSION OF THE GOVERNING COUNCIL OF THE UNITED NATIONS COMPENSATION COMMISSION

CRITERIA FOR EXPEDITED PROCESSING OF URGENT CLAIMS

1. The following criteria will govern the submission of the most urgent claims pursuant to resolution 687 (1991) for the first categories to be considered by the Commission. It provides for simple and expedited procedures by which Governments may submit consolidated claims and receive payments on behalf of the many individuals who suffered personal losses as a result of the invasion and occupation of Kuwait. For a great many persons these procedures would provide prompt compensation in full; for others they will provide substantial interim relief while their larger or more complex claims are being processed, including those suffering business losses.

2. These criteria are without prejudice to future Council decisions with respect to criteria for other categories of claims, which will be approved separately as promptly as possible, with expert advice from Commissioners as may be required.

3. The following criteria are not intended to resolve every issue that may arise with respect to these claims. Rather, they are intended to provide sufficient guidance to enable Governments to prepare consolidated claims submissions. It will likely be necessary for the Council to make further decisions on the processing of claims after receiving expert advice where needed.

4. Each Government may submit one or more consolidated claims for each category established by the Council. Thus, each Government may make separate consolidated submissions covering claims in each of the categories set forth below; and it may later submit separate consolidated claims for each additional category to be established by the Council.

GE.91-71757/6864a

S/AC.26/1991/1
page 2

5. The Council will promptly establish criteria for additional categories of claims, to permit consolidated submissions by Governments for all losses covered by paragraph 16 of resolution 687 (1991). Business losses of individuals may be part of consolidated claims under the expedited procedures set forth below. The Council will provide further advice on an urgent basis as to the types of business losses eligible for consideration under the expedited procedures. Business losses of corporations and other legal entities will be covered in other criteria to be established. The Council will also separately consider claims on behalf of third parties, such as Governments, insurance companies, relief agencies and employers, which have made payments or provided relief to persons suffering compensable losses.

6. The Council will consider promptly, after receiving expert advice, the circumstances in which claims for mental pain and anguish may be admitted, the amounts to be awarded, and the limits to be imposed thereon.

7. The Council will separately examine the question of the eligibility or otherwise of claims by or in respect of members of the allied coalition armed forces; the Executive Secretary will have available, inter alia, the provisions of the relevant national legislation of the Governments concerned.

8. The Commission will process the claims in the initial categories in paragraphs 10 to 16 on an expedited basis. While decisions on the precise method of processing these claims will be made at a later stage, the following steps are contemplated. As the claims are received they would be submitted to a panel of Commissioners for review within a set time limit. If, as expected, the volume of claims in these categories is large, the Commissioners would be instructed to adopt expedited procedures to process them, such as checking individual claims on a sample basis, with further verification only if circumstances warranted. The Commissioners would be asked to report to the Council on the claims received and the amount recommended for the claims submitted by each Government. The Council would then decide on the total amount to be allocated to each Government. To the extent necessary, the Council would seek expert advice (for example, on what constitutes serious personal injury) at any stage of the process.

9. As contributions are made to the Fund, the Council will allocate those funds among the various categories of claims. If resources of the Fund are insufficient with respect to all claims processed to date, pro rata payments would be made to Governments periodically as funds become available. The Council will decide on the priority for payment of various categories of claims.

PAYMENT OF FIXED AMOUNTS

10. These payments are available with respect to any person who, as a result of Iraq's unlawful invasion and occupation of Kuwait: (a) departed from Iraq or Kuwait during the period of 2 August 1990 to 2 March 1991; (b) suffered serious personal injury; or (c) whose spouse, child or parent died.

11. In the case of departures, $2,500 will be provided where there is simple documentation of the fact and date of departure from Iraq or Kuwait. Documentation of the actual amount of loss will not be required. Claims submitted under this procedure for departure from Iraq or Kuwait cannot be

resubmitted for a greater amount in any other category. If the loss in question was greater than $2,500 and can be documented, it may instead be submitted under paragraph`14 and in other appropriate categories.

12. In addition, in the case of serious personal injury not resulting in death, $2,500 will be provided where there is simple documentation of the fact and date of the injury; and in the case of death, $2,500 will be provided where there is simple documentation of the death and family relationship. Documentation of the actual amount of loss resulting from the death or injury will not be required. If the actual loss in question was greater than $2,500, these payments will be treated as interim relief, and claims for additional amounts may also be submitted under paragraph`14 and in other appropriate categories.

13. These amounts are payable cumulatively where more than one situation applies with respect to a particular person. However, no more than $10,000 will be paid for death, and no more than $5,000 for departure, with respect to any one family (consisting of any person and his or her spouse, children and parents).

CONSIDERATION OF CLAIMS FOR UP TO $100,000
OF ACTUAL LOSSES PER PERSON

14. These payments are available with respect to death or personal injury, or losses of income, support, housing or personal property, or medical expenses or costs of departure, as a result of Iraq's unlawful invasion and occupation of Kuwait. The Commission will give expedited priority consideration to claims for such losses up to $100,000 per person.

15. (a) Such claims must be documented by appropriate evidence of the circumstances and the amount of the claimed loss. The evidence required will be the reasonable minimum that is appropriate under the circumstances involved, and a lesser degree of documentary evidence would ordinarily be required for smaller claims, such as those below $20,000.

(b) If the loss in question was greater than $100,000, claims for additional amounts may also be submitted in other appropriate categories. Criteria for the submission of claims in excess of $100,000 will be approved separately. Claims larger than $100,000 may be submitted in their entirety at a later date under those separate procedures, or the first $100,000 may be submitted at this time and the remainder separately.

16. Compensation will not be provided for losses suffered as a result of the trade embargo and related measures, nor will costs of attorneys' fees or other expenses for claims preparation be compensated under this category. Any compensation, whether in funds or in kind, already received from any source will be deducted from the total amount of losses suffered.

REQUIREMENTS APPLICABLE UNDER BOTH CATEGORIES

17. Claims will not be considered on behalf of Iraqi nationals who do not have bona fide nationality of any other State.

18. Claims must be for death, personal injury or other direct loss to individuals as a result of Iraq's unlawful invasion and occupation of Kuwait. This will include any loss suffered as a result of:

(a) military operations or threat of military action by either side during the period 2 August 1990 to 2 March 1991;

(b) departure from or inability to leave Iraq or Kuwait (or a decision not to return) during that period;

(c) actions by officials, employees or agents of the Government of Iraq or its controlled entities during that period in connection with the invasion or occupation;

(d) the breakdown of civil order in Kuwait or Iraq during that period; or

(e) hostage-taking or other illegal detention.

19. Claims will be submitted by Governments. Each Government will normally submit claims on behalf of its nationals; each Government may, in its discretion, also submit the claims of other persons resident in its territory. In addition, the Council may request an appropriate person, authority or body to submit claims on behalf of persons who are not in a position to have their claims submitted by a Government. Each Government shall make one or more consolidated submissions of all such claims for each category. The Council encourages the submission of such claims within six months from the date on which the Executive Secretary circulates to Governments the claims forms described below; and the Commission will thereupon give consideration to such claims as provided herein. The Council will consider at a later time the period within which all such claims must be submitted.

20. Each consolidated claim must include:

(a) a signed statement by each individual covered containing:

(i) his or her name and address, and any passport number or other identifying national number;

(ii) for claims under paragraph 14, the amount, type, and reason for each element of the loss, and any compensation, whether in funds or in kind already received from any source for the claim asserted;

(iii) any documents evidencing the matters set forth in the definition of each category, as well as the items set forth in the preceding subparagraph; and

(iv) his or her affirmation that the foregoing information is correct, and that no other claim for the same loss has been submitted to the Commission;

(b) the affirmation of the Government submitting the claim that, to the best of the information available to it, the individuals in question are its nationals or residents, and the affirmation of the Government or of the person, authority or body as referred to in paragraph`19 that it has no reason to believe that the information stated is incorrect.

21. The Executive Secretary (or a Commissioner) will prepare and the Executive Secretary will distribute a standard form for submission of claims within each category, incorporating the above elements in a clear and concise manner. Except as may otherwise be agreed between the Executive Secretary and the Government in question, claims will be submitted to the Executive Secretary by Governments or by persons, authorities or bodies as referred to in paragraph`19 on the standard form and must include the information in an official language of the United`Nations. Each Government may adopt such procedures as it finds appropriate in preparing its consolidated claim. The Executive Secretary (or a Commissioner) will be available to answer questions or provide assistance to any Governments which may request it.

UNITED
NATIONS

S

Security Council

Distr.
GENERAL

S/AC.26/1992/9
6 March 1992

Original: ENGLISH

UNITED NATIONS
COMPENSATION COMMISSION
GOVERNING COUNCIL
Resumed Fourth Session
Geneva, 6 March 1992

Decision taken by the Governing Council of the United Nations Compensation Commission during the resumed Fourth Session, at the 23rd meeting, held on 6th March 1992

Propositions and Conclusions on Compensation for Business Losses: Types of Damages and Their Valuation

1. The propositions and conclusions contained in this Decision sha apply to compensation for the loss of earnings or profits and oth business losses covered by Security Council resolution 687 (1991).

2. The basic premise underlying all of the findings concerni business losses is that, pursuant to paragraph 16 of Security Counc resolution 687 (1991), Iraq "is liable under international law for a direct loss, damage, including environmental damage and the depleti of natural resources, or injury to foreign Governments, nationals a corporations as a result of Iraq's unlawful invasion and occupati of Kuwait".

3. This Decision does not attempt to describe all of the conceivab factual and legal situations resulting from Iraq's invasion a occupation of Kuwait. Bearing in mind Security Council resolution 6 (1991), other types of losses may have been suffered, and they a eligible for compensation if they result from Iraq's invasion a occupation of Kuwait. Ultimately, it will be up to the Commissione to identify the applicable principles and apply them to t circumstances of particular cases.

/.....

GE.92-70136

S/AC.26/1992/9
page 2

4. The propositions and conclusions contained in this Decision are not intended to be a comprehensive statement of relevant principles. The Governing Council will review the matter and will provide further guidance concerning business losses as required in the future. In particular, the Governing Council will request the Secretariat to consider the question of steps which might be taken to protect against multiple recovery of compensation by claimants, or to confirm that claimants have attempted to avail themselves of particular possible sources of recovery, as a prerequisite to relief from the Commission.

5. When reference is made herein to corporations and other legal entities, it is understood that such corporations or other legal entities may be either publicly or privately owned enterprises.

6. The trade embargo and related measures*, and the economic situation caused thereby, will not be accepted as the basis for compensation. Compensation will be provided to the extent that Iraq's unlawful invasion and occupation of Kuwait constituted a cause of direct loss, damage or injury which is separate and distinct from the trade embargo and related measures. (Where, for example, the full extent of the loss, damage or injury arose as a direct result of Iraq's unlawful invasion and occupation of Kuwait, it should be compensated notwithstanding the fact that it may also be attributable to the trade embargo and related measures). The total amount of compensable losses will be reduced to the extent that those losses could reasonably have been avoided. Further guidance on the matters dealt with in this paragraph will be provided by the Governing Council for the use of the Commissioners when assessing claims.

* The trade embargo and related measures refers to the prohibitions in United Nations Security Council Resolution 661 (1990) and relevant subsequent resolutions and the measures taken by states pursuant thereto.

I. LOSSES IN CONNECTION WITH CONTRACTS OR PAST BUSINESS PRACTI

A) Contracts

7. The following general conclusions apply with regard to Iraq's liability for contract losses.

Contracts with Iraq

8. Where Iraq itself was a contracting party and breached its contractual obligations, Iraq is liable under general contract law to compensate for all actual losses suffered by the other contracting party, including, inter alia, losses relating to specially manufactured goods. Future lost profits may be compensable in such a case if they can be calculated under the contract with reasonable certainty. An alternative measure of damages may apply where a governing contract specifically provides for a particular measure, except that the amount of compensation provided should not exceed the loss actually suffered. Breaches of contract not resulting from the invasion and occupation of Kuwait are not within the jurisdiction of the Commission.

9. Where Iraq did not breach a contract to which it was a party, but continuation of the contract became impossible for the other party as a result of Iraq's invasion and occupation of Kuwait, Iraq is liable for any direct loss the other party suffered as a result, including lost profits. In such a situation, Iraq should not be allowed to invoke *force majeure* or similar contract provisions, or general principles of contract excuse, to avoid its liability.

Contracts where Iraq is not a party

10. Where losses have been suffered in connection with contracts to which Iraq was not a party, the following conclusions apply. Iraq is responsible for the losses that have resulted from the invasion and occupation of Kuwait. A relevant consideration may be whether the contracting parties could resume the contract after the lifting of the embargo against Kuwait, and whether they have in fact resumed the contract. Iraq principally cannot be relieved from its responsibility by *force majeure* provisions of contracts to which it is not a party or contract excuse rules of other applicable laws.

B) Past business practice

11. Where a loss has been suffered relating to a transaction that has been part of a business practice or course of dealing, Iraq is liable according to the principles that apply to contract losses. No liability exists for losses related to transactions that were only expected to take place based on a previous course of dealing.

II. LOSSES RELATING TO TANGIBLE ASSETS

12. Where direct losses were suffered as a result of Iraq's invasion and occupation of Kuwait with respect to tangible assets, Iraq is liable for compensation. Typical actions of this kind would have been expropriation, removal, theft or destruction of particular items of property by Iraqi authorities. Whether the taking of property was lawful or not is not relevant for Iraq's liability if it did not provide for compensation.

13. In a case where business property had been lost because it had been left unguarded by company personnel departing due to the situation in Iraq and Kuwait, such loss may be considered as resulting directly from the invasion and occupation.

14. On the other hand, losses that occurred because company personnel was detained by Iraqi authorities, must clearly be considered a direct result. In this context, it is relevant to note the Hague Regulations on Land Warfare annexed to Conventions II of 1899 and IV of 1907 respecting the Laws and Customs of War on Land, which require that an occupying power has to restore and to ensure public order and safety as far as possible (Hague Regulations, Article 43).

15. Depending on the type of asset and the circumstances of the case, one of several valuation methods may be used. Methods typically used to value tangible assets are book value and replacement value. *Book value* is considered to mean value at which an asset is carried on a balance sheet. Book value at any time is cost of an item minus accumulated depreciation. *Replacement value* is considered to mean the amount required to obtain an asset of the same kind and status as the asset damaged or lost. Replacement value would not normally allow for replacement of an old item with a new one.

III. LOSSES RELATING TO INCOME-PRODUCING PROPERTIES

16. The following general conclusions apply with regard to losses suffered as a result of Iraq's invasion and occupation of Kuwait in connection with income-producing properties. These include various kinds of businesses whose value is determined not only by the value of their individual assets but also by the greater value they possess due to their capacity to generate income. The conclusions are based on the premise that the business affected was a going concern, i.e. it had the capacity to continue to operate and generate income in the future.

17. In principle, Iraq is liable to compensate for the loss of a business or commercial entity as a whole resulting from Iraq's invasion and occupation of Kuwait. In the event that the business has been rebuilt and resumed, or that it could reasonably have been expected that the business could have been rebuilt and resumed, compensation may only be claimed for the loss suffered during the relevant period.

18. For the valuation of income-producing properties there are several alternative concepts. One is to measure by reference to costs, which leads to the determination of book value. Another is to determine the value of the property as a going concern. This is often done by reference to the market value of similar properties. Where such market value cannot be ascertained, the economic or current value of that asset can be ascertained by the *discounted cash flow (DCF)* method or by the *price/earnings (P/E)* method. The DCF method calculates the value at one specified time of cash flows that are to be received at a different time by discounting the yearly net cash flows to present value, with the discount rate including cost of capital and risk components. The price/earnings method takes as a basis past periods' business results and then capitalises them by the application of a multiple (P/E ratio) which reflects expectations about future performance and growth, or lack of it.

19. In principle, the economic value of a business may include loss of future earnings and profits where they can be ascertained with reasonable certainty. In the case of the loss of businesses and their earning capacity resulting from the invasion and occupation of Kuwait, it can be expected that a number of such businesses can be or could have been rebuilt and resumed. The method of a valuation should therefore be one that focuses on past performance rather than on forecasts and projections into the future. Compensation should be provided if the loss can be ascertained with reasonable certainty based on prior earnings or profits. For example, the loss of any earnings or profits during the relevant time period could be calculated by a multiple of past earnings and profits corresponding to that time period.

UNITED NATIONS

S

Security Council

Distr.
GENERAL

S/AC.26/1991/7/Rev.1
17 March 1992

Original: ENGLISH

UNITED NATIONS COMPENSATION COMMISSION
GOVERNING COUNCIL
Fifth Session
Geneva, 16-20 March 1992

Decision taken by the Governing Council of the United Nations Compensation Commission during its third session, at the 18th meeting, held on 28 November 1991, as revised at the 24th meeting held on 16 March 1992

Criteria for additional Categories of Claims

I. Criteria for processing of claims of individuals not otherwise covered

1. The following criteria will govern the submission of all claims of individuals not filed under the criteria adopted by the Governing Council on 2 August 1991, pursuant to resolution 687 (1991).

2. The following criteria are not intended to resolve every issue that may arise with respect to these claims. Rather, they are intended to provide sufficient guidance to enable Governments to prepare consolidated claims submissions.

3. The Commission will process the claims as expeditiously as possible. While decisions on the precise method of processing these claims will be made at a later stage the following steps are contemplated. The Secretariat will make a preliminary assessment of the claims to determine whether they meet the formal requirements established by the Governing Council. The claims would then be submitted to a panel or panels of Commissioners for review within a set time-limit. The Commissioners would be instructed to utilize different procedures appropriate to the character, amount and subject-matter of particular types of claims. In so far as possible, claims with significant common legal or factual issues should be processed together. The Commissioners would be asked to report to the Council on the claims received and the amount recommended for the claims submitted by each Government. The Council would then decide on the total amount to be allocated to each Government. The Council may decide to refer unusually large or complex claims to panels of Commissioners for detailed review, possibly involving additional written submissions and oral proceedings. In such a case, the individual would be allowed to present his or her case directly to the panel.

4. As contributions are made to the Fund, the Council will allocate those funds

among the various categories of claims. If resources of the Fund are insuffici with respect to all claims processed to date, pro rata payments would be made t Governments periodically as funds become available. The Council will decide on the priority for payment of various categories of claims.

5. Claims may be submitted under this category for the loss of earnings or profits; the Commission will consider at a later time the circumstances in whic such claims may be admitted, the amounts to be awarded, and the limits to be imposed thereon.

Claims covered

6. These payments are available with respect to any direct loss, damage, or injury (including death) to individuals as a result of Iraq's unlawful invasion and occupation of Kuwait. This will include any loss suffered as a result of:

(a) Military operations or threat of military action by either side durin the period 2 August 1990 to 2 March 1991;

(b) Departure from or inability to leave Iraq or Kuwait (or a decision no to return) during that period;

(c) Actions by officials, employees or agents of the Government of Iraq o its controlled entities during that period in connection with the invasion or occupation;

(d) The breakdown of civil order in Kuwait or Iraq during that period; or

(e) Hostage-taking or other illegal detention.

7. These payments are available with respect to individuals who claim losses excess of those compensable under claim forms B or C. These payments are also available with respect to individuals who have chosen not to file under claim f A, B, or C because their losses exceed $100,000. In addition, these payments a available to reimburse payments made or relief provided by individuals to other for example, to employees or to others pursuant to contractual obligations - fo losses covered by any of the criteria adopted by the Council.

8. Since these claims may be for substantial amounts, they must be supported documentary and other appropriate evidence sufficient to demonstrate the circumstances and the amount of the claimed loss.

9. Direct losses as a result of Iraq's unlawful invasion and occupation of Kuwait are eligible for compensation. Compensation will not be provided for losses suffered as a result of the trade embargo and related measures. Further guidance will be provided on the interpretation and application of this paragra

10. Any compensation, whether in funds or in kind, already received from any source will be deducted from the total amount of losses suffered.

Submission of claims

11. Claims will not be considered on behalf of Iraqi nationals who do not have bona fide nationality of any other State.

12. Claims will be submitted by Governments. Each Government may submit claims on behalf of its nationals, and may in its discretion also submit the claims of other persons resident in its territory. In addition, the Council may request an appropriate person, authority, or body to submit claims on behalf of persons who are not in a position to have their claims submitted by a Government.

13. Each consolidated claim must include:

(a) For each separate claim, a signed statement by each individual covered containing:

(i) his or her name and address, and any passport number or other identifying national number;

(ii) a description of and documents evidencing the amount, type, and reason for each element of the loss;

(iii) identification of any compensation, whether in funds or in kind, already received from any source for the claim asserted;

(iv) his or her affirmation that the foregoing information is correct, and that no other claim for the same loss has been submitted to the Commission;

(v) a copy of any previously submitted individual claim; and

(b) The affirmation of the Government submitting the claim that, to the best of the information available to it, the individuals in question are its nationals or residents, and the affirmation of the Government or of the person, authority, or body as referred to in paragraph 12 that it has no reason to believe that the information stated is incorrect.

14. The Executive Secretary (or a Commissioner) will prepare and the Executive Secretary will distribute a standard form for submission of these claims, incorporating the above elements in a clear and concise manner. Except as may otherwise be agreed between the Executive Secretary and the Government in question, claims will be submitted to the Executive Secretary by Governments or by persons, authorities, or bodies as referred to in paragraph 12 on the standard form and must include the information in an official language of the United Nations. Each Government may adopt such procedures as it finds appropriate in preparing its claims. The Executive Secretary (or a Commissioner) will be available to answer questions or provide assistance to any Governments which may request it.

15. Governments must submit all claims on behalf of individuals within one year of the date on which the Executive Secretary circulates these claims forms. The Council encourages the submission of such claims within six months from the date on which the Executive Secretary circulates to Governments the claims forms; and the Commission will thereupon give consideration to such claims as provided herein.

II. Criteria for processing claims of corporations and other entities

16. The following criteria will govern the submission of claims of corporations, other private legal entities and public-sector enterprises (hereinafter referred to as "corporations and other entities") pursuant to resolution 687 (1991).

17. The following criteria are not intended to resolve every issue that may ar with respect to these claims. Rather, they are intended to provide sufficient guidance to enable Governments to prepare consolidated claims submissions.

18. The Commission will process the claims as expeditiously as possible. Whil decisions on the precise method of processing these claims will be made at a la stage the following steps are contemplated. The Secretariat will make a preliminary assessment of the claims to determine whether they meet the formal requirements established by the Governing Council. The claims would then be submitted to a panel or panels of Commissioners for review within a set time-limit. The Commissioners would be instructed to utilize different procedu appropriate to the character, amount and subject-matter of particular types of claims. In so far as possible, claims with significant common legal or factual issues should be processed together. The Commissioners would be asked to repor to the Council on the claims received and the amount recommended for the claims submitted by each Government. The Council would then decide on the total amoun to be allocated to each Government. The Council may decide to refer unusually large or complex claims to panels of Commissioners for detailed review, possibl involving additional written submissions and oral proceedings. In such a case, the entity would be allowed to present its case directly to the panel.

19. As contributions are made to the Fund, the Council will allocate those fun among the various categories of claims. If resources of the Fund are insuffici with respect to all claims processed to date, pro rata payments would be made t Governments periodically as funds become available. The Council will decide on the priority for payment of various categories of claims.

20. Claims may be submitted under this category for the loss of earnings or profits; the Commission will consider at a later time the circumstances under which such claims may be admitted, the amounts to be awarded, and the limits to imposed thereon.

Claims covered

21. These payments are available with respect to any direct loss, damage, or injury to corporations and other entities as a result of Iraq's unlawful invasion and occupation of Kuwait. This will include any loss suffered as a result of:

(a) Military operations or threat of military action by either side during the period 2 August 1990 to 2 March 1991;

(b) Departure of persons from or their inability to leave Iraq or Kuwait (or a decision not to return) during that period;

(c) Actions by officials, employees or agents of the Government of Iraq or its controlled entities during that period in connection with the invasion or occupation;

(d) The breakdown of civil order in Kuwait or Iraq during that period; or

(e) Hostage-taking or other illegal detention.

22. These payments are available to reimburse payments made or relief provided by corporations or other entities to others - for example, to employees, or to others pursuant to contractual obligations - for losses covered by any of the criteria adopted by the Council.

23. Since these claims may be for substantial amounts, they must be supported by documentary and other appropriate evidence sufficient to demonstrate the circumstances and the amount of the claimed loss.

24. Direct losses as a result of Iraq's unlawful invasion and occupation of Kuwait are eligible for compensation. Compensation will not be provided for losses suffered as a result of the trade embargo and related measures. Further guidance will be provided on the interpretation and application of this paragraph.

25. Any compensation, whether in funds or in kind, already received from any source will be deducted from the total amount of losses suffered.

Submission of claims

26. Each Government may submit claims on behalf of corporations or other entities that, on the date on which the claim arose, were incorporated or organized under its law. Claims may be submitted on behalf of a corporation or other entity by only one Government. A corporation or other entity would be required to request the State of its incorporation or organization to submit its claim to the Commission. In the case of a corporation or other private legal entity whose State of incorporation or organization fails to submit, within the deadline established in paragraph 29, such claims falling within the applicable criteria, the corporation or other private legal entity may itself make a claim to the Commission within three months thereafter. It

S/AC.26/1991/7/Rev.1
page 6

must submit at the same time an explanation as to why its claim is not being submitted by a Government, together with the relevant information specified in paragraph 27. In such a case, any award of the Commission will be paid directly to the corporation or other private legal entity.

27. Each consolidated claim must include:

(a) For each separate claim, a signed statement by an authorized official c each corporation or other entity covered containing:

(i) documents evidencing the name, address and place of incorporation or organization of the entity;

(ii) a general description of the legal structure of the entity;

(iii) a description of and documents evidencing the amount, type, and reason for each element of the loss;

(iv) identification of any compensation, whether in funds or in kind, already received from any source for the claim asserted;

(v) his or her name and address and affirmation that the foregoing information is correct, and that no other claim for the same loss has been submitted to the Commission;

(b) The affirmation of the Government submitting the claim that, to the bes of the information available to it, the entities in question are incorporated or organized under its law and the affirmation of the Government that it has no reason to believe that the information stated is incorrect.

28. The Executive Secretary (or a Commissioner) will prepare and the Executive Secretary will distribute a standard form for submission of these claims, incorporating the above elements in a clear and concise manner. Except as may otherwise be agreed between the Executive Secretary and the Government in question, claims will be submitted to the Executive Secretary by Governments on the standard form and must include the information in an official language of the United Nations. Each Government may adopt such procedures as it finds appropriat in preparing its claims. The Executive Secretary (or a Commissioner) will be available to answer questions or provide assistance to any Governments which may request it.

29. Governments must submit all claims on behalf of corporations or other entities within one year of the date the Executive Secretary circulates the claim forms. The Council encourages the submission of such claims within six months from the date on which the Executive Secretary circulates to Governments the claims forms; and the Commission will thereupon give consideration to such claims as provided herein.

III. Criteria for processing claims of governments and international organizations

30. The following criteria will govern the submission of claims of Governments and international organizations pursuant to resolution 687 (1991). Each Government will submit claims of its own and those of its political subdivisions, or any agency, ministry, instrumentality, or entity controlled by it.

31. The following criteria are not intended to resolve every issue that may arise with respect to these claims. Rather, they are intended to provide sufficient guidance to enable Governments and international organizations to prepare consolidated claims submissions.

32. The Commission will process the claims as expeditiously as possible. While decisions on the precise method of processing these claims will be made at a later stage the following steps are contemplated. The Secretariat will make a preliminary assessment of the claims to determine whether they meet the formal requirements established by the Governing Council. The claims would then be submitted to a panel or panels of Commissioners for review within a set time-limit. The Commissioners would be instructed to utilize different procedures appropriate to the character, amount and subject-matter of particular types of claims. In so far as possible, claims with significant common legal or factual issues should be processed together. The Commissioners would be asked to report to the Council on the claims received and the amount recommended for the claims submitted by each Government. The Council would then decide on the total amount to be allocated to each Government. The Council may decide to refer unusually large or complex claims to panels of Commissioners for detailed review, possibly involving additional written submissions and oral proceedings. In such a case, when an international organization is involved, it would be allowed to present its case directly to the panel.

33. As contributions are made to the Fund, the Council will allocate those funds among the various categories of claims. If resources of the Fund are insufficient with respect to all claims processed to date, pro rata payments would be made to Governments periodically as funds become available. The Council will decide on the priority for payment of various categories of claims.

Claims covered

34. These payments are available with respect to any direct loss, damage, or injury to Governments or international organizations as a result of Iraq's unlawful invasion and occupation of Kuwait. This will include any loss suffered as a result of:

(a) Military operations or threat of military action by either side during the period 2 August 1990 to 2 March 1991;

(b) Departure of persons from or their inability to leave Iraq or Kuwait (or a decision not to return) during that period;

(c) Actions by officials, employees or agents of the Government of Iraq or its controlled entities during that period in connection with the invasion or occupation;

(d) The breakdown of civil order in Kuwait or Iraq during that period; or

(e) Hostage-taking or other illegal detention.

35. These payments are available with respect to direct environmental damage and the depletion of natural resources as a result of Iraq's unlawful invasion and occupation of Kuwait. This will include losses or expenses resulting from:

(a) Abatement and prevention of environmental damage, including expenses directly relating to fighting oil fires and stemming the flow of oil in coastal

S/AC.26/1991/7/Rev.1
page 8

and international waters;

(b) Reasonable measures already taken to clean and restore the environment or future measures which can be documented as reasonably necessary to clean and restore the environment;

(c) Reasonable monitoring and assessment of the environmental damage for t purposes of evaluating and abating the harm and restoring the environment;

(d) Reasonable monitoring of public health and performing medical screenir for the purposes of investigation and combating increased health risks as a resu of the environmental damage; and

(e) Depletion of or damage to natural resources.

36. These payments will include loss of or damage to property of a Government, well as losses and costs incurred by a Government in evacuating its nationals fr Iraq or Kuwait. These payments are also available to reimburse payments made or relief provided by Governments or international organizations to others - for example to nationals, residents or employees or to others pursuant to contractua obligations - for losses covered by any of the criteria adopted by the Council.

37. Since these claims will be for substantial amounts, they must be supported documentary and other appropriate evidence sufficient to demonstrate the circumstances and the amount of the claimed loss.

38. Direct losses as a result of Iraq's unlawful invasion and occupation of Kuwait are eligible for compensation. Compensation will not be provided for losses suffered as a result of the trade embargo and related measures. Further guidance will be provided on the interpretation and application of this paragrap

39. Any compensation, whether in funds or in kind, already received from any source will be deducted from the total amount of losses suffered.

Submission of claims

40. Each consolidated claim must include:

(a) For each separate claim, a signed statement by an authorized official of the Government or international organization containing:

(i) his or her name and address, and government agency instrumentality, or ministry or controlled entity, or the international organization, with which associated;

(ii) a description of and documents evidencing the amount, type, and reason for each element of the loss;

(iii) identification of any compensation, whether in funds or in kind, already received from any source for the claim asserted;

(iv) his or her affirmation that the foregoing information is correct, and that no other claim for the same loss has been submitted to the Commission;

(b) The affirmation of the Government or international organization submitting the consolidated claim that to the best of the information available to it, it has no reason to believe that the information stated is incorrect.

41. The Executive Secretary (or a Commissioner) will prepare and the Executive Secretary will distribute a standard form for submission of claims, incorporating the above elements in a clear and concise manner. Except as may otherwise be agreed between the Executive Secretary and the Government or international organization in question, claims will be submitted to the Executive Secretary on the standard form and must include the information in an official language of the United Nations. The Executive Secretary (or a Commissioner) will be available to answer questions or provide assistance to any Governments or international organizations which may request it.

42. Governments and international organizations must submit all claims within one year of the date on which the Executive Secretary circulates the standard form. The Council encourages the submission of such claims within six months from the date on which the Executive Secretary circulates to Governments and international organizations the claims forms; and the Commission will thereupon give consideration to such claims as provided herein.

UNITED NATIONS

S

Security Council

Distr.
GENERAL

S/AC.26/1992/10
26 June 1992

Original: ENGLISH

UNITED NATIONS
COMPENSATION COMMISSION

GOVERNING COUNCIL
Sixth session
Geneva, 22-26 June 1992

Decision taken by the Governing Council of the United Nations Compensation Commission at the 27th meeting, Sixth session held on 26 June 1992

The Governing Council decides:

To approve the Provisional Rules for Claims Procedure the text of which is annexed to the present decision.

Annex

PROVISIONAL RULES FOR CLAIMS PROCEDURE

I) GENERAL PROVISIONS

Article 1. Use of Terms

The following definitions apply for the purpose of these Rules:

1) "Commission" means the United Nations Compensation Commission.

2) "Compensation Fund" or "Fund" means the United Nations Compensation Fund, created by paragraph 18 of Security Council resolution 687 (1991) and established by paragraph 3 of Security Council resolution 692 (1991) in accordance with section I of the Secretary-General's Report (S/22559) dated 2 May 1991.

3) "Secretary-General" means the Secretary-General of the United Nations.

4) "Governing Council" or "Council" means the Governing Council of the Commission.

5) "Commissioners" means experts appointed by the Governing Council for the verification and evaluation of claims.

6) "Executive Secretary" means the Executive Secretary of the Commission and includes any Deputy of, or other person, authorized by the Executive Secretary.

7) "Secretariat" means the Secretariat of the Commission.

8) "Standard Forms" means claim forms prepared and distributed to Governments by the Executive Secretary for claims under claims criteria adopted by the Governing Council.

/...

9) "Claim Forms" means standard forms and any other form agreed between the Executive Secretary and the Government or international organization in question for filing claims.

10) "Rules" means the Commission's Provisional Rules for Claims Procedure.

11) "Criteria" means Criteria for Expedited Processing of Urgent Claims (Governing Council's decision No. S/AC.26/1991/ dated 2 August 1991), and Criteria for Additional Categories of Claims (Governing Council's decision No. S/AC.26/1991/7 dated 4 December 1991) as well as any other criteria that the Governing Council may adopt.

12) "Claimant" means any individual, corporation or other private legal entity, public sector entity, Government or international organization that files a claim with the Commission.

13) "Person or Body" means an individual, corporation or other private legal entity, public sector entity, Government, or international organization.

14) "International Organization" means an international organization of States.

15) "Documents" means all submissions and evidence presented by a claimant in support of a claim, in whatever form, including Statements of Claim in categories E and F.

16) "Database" means computerized information, pertaining to individual claimants and claims, kept by the Commission to assist in the processing of claims.

S/AC.26/1992/10
Page 4

Article 2. Scope of the Rules

These Rules apply to processing of claims submitted to the Commission under the criteria adopted by the Governing Council.

Article 3. Calculation of Periods of Time

For the purposes of calculating a period of time under these Rules, such period shall begin to run on the day following the day when the document is received or a notification is made. If the last day of such period is an official holiday or a non-business day at the headquarters of the Commission, the period is extended until the first business day that follows. Official holidays and non-business days occurring during the running of the period of time are included in calculating the period. The Executive Secretary will issue a list of such days.

II) SUBMISSION AND FILING OF CLAIMS

Article 4. Submission of Claims

1) Claim forms and documents are to be submitted to the Commission at the Secretariat's headquarters (Palais des Nations, Villa La Pelouse, Geneva, Switzerland).

2) Claim forms shall be deemed to have been submitted when they are physically delivered to and received by the Secretariat.

Article 5. Who May Submit Claims

1) Governments and international organizations are entitled to submit claims to the Commission.

a) A Government may submit claims on behalf of its nationals and, at its discretion, of other persons resident in its territory. In the case of Governments existing in the territory of a former federal state, one such Government may submit claims on behalf of nationals, corporations or other entities of another such Government, if both Governments agree.

b) A Government may submit claims on behalf of corporations or other entities that, on the date on which the claim arose, were incorporated or organized under the law of that State. If the Governments concerned agree, one Government may submit claims in respect of joint ventures on behalf of the nationals, corporations or other entities of other Governments.

c) Claims may be submitted on behalf of an individual, corporation or other entity by only one Government.

d) International organizations may submit claims only on their own behalf.

2) An appropriate person, authority, or body appointed by the Governing Council may submit claims on behalf of persons who are not in a position to have their claims submitted by a Government.

3) A corporation or other private legal entity is required to request the State of its incorporation or organization to submit its claim to the Commission. In the case of a corporation or other private legal entity whose State of incorporation or organization fails to submit, within the time-limit established by the Governing Council, such claims falling within the applicable criteria, the corporation or other private legal entity may itself make a claim to the Commission within three months thereafter. It must provide at the same time an explanation as to why its claim is not being submitted by a Government.

Article 6. Claim Forms and Language

1) Except as may otherwise be agreed between the Executive Secretary and the Government or international organization in question, claims must be submitted on the standard forms prepared and distributed by the Secretariat.

2) Due to the fact that the Commission's computerized software and database system, which is technically required for the processing of a large number of claims, has been designed in English, the working language of the claims procedure before the Commission will be English.

3) Claim forms can be submitted in any of the official languages of the United Nations. However, since English is the working language of the claims procedure and of the Commission's computerized database, in cases where claim forms are not submitted in English, an English translation of the form must be provided. The translation as submitted, will serve as the basis for the evaluation of the claim.

4) With respect to claims in categories A, B and C, the documents supporting the claims are not required to be translated into English at the stage of the submission of the claims. The Secretariat, on the basis of methods adopted for processing and evaluation of claims, will notify each Government as to the extent of the translation required and the time-limit for providing it.

5) With respect to claims in categories D, E and F, all documents supporting the claims must also be submitted in English or be accompanied by an English translation.

6) In the case of oral proceedings, the Executive Secretary shall arrange for interpretation as necessary into and from other official languages of the United Nations.

Article 7. Format of Claims

1) Claim forms in category A must be submitted only in the computer format distributed by the Secretariat. Governments will maintain custody of the original paper copies of Form A and supporting documents and will make them available to the Commission upon request.

2) Claim forms and documents in all other categories must be submitted on paper. In addition to filing claims in these categories on paper, Governments may also submit them in a computer format.

3) All claim forms and documents filed with the Commission on paper are to be submitted on paper 8 1/2 inches x 11 inches or on A-4 size paper (21 cm x 29.5 cm) or on paper no larger than A-4. If a document cannot conveniently be reproduced on paper no larger than A-4, it is to be folded to A-4 size, unless the Executive Secretary agrees otherwise in special circumstances.

4) Claims and documents filed with the Commission in a computer format are to be submitted on MS/DOS or UNIX compatible formats, or in such other format as may be agreed to by the Executive Secretary.

Article 8. Copies

1) Except as otherwise agreed to by the Executive Secretary, claim forms and documents must be submitted with the following number of copies:

For category A:	3 copies of micro floppy disk
For categories B & C:	1 original and 2 copies
For D & other categories:	1 original and 8 copies

2) The Secretariat, or the Commissioners, may request additional copies or accept a smaller number in exceptional circumstances.

Article 9. Representatives

For the purpose of these Rules, all communications between the Commission's Secretariat and a Government concerning claims shall take place through its Permanent Mission in Geneva. Further, except in cases where a specially authorized representative is designated by a Government and notified to the Executive Secretary, the head of the Permanent Mission of a Government shall be considered as its representative before the Commission. Governments that do not maintain Permanent Missions in Geneva and international organizations shall notify the name of their duly authorized representatives to the Executive Secretary.

Article 10. <u>The Registry</u>

A registry will be set up within the Secretariat. A member of the Secretariat will be designated by the Executive Secretary as Registry Officer. The Registry Officer will receive the claims and register them.

Article 11. <u>Receipt of Claims</u>

1) Upon the submission of a claim, the Registry Officer will issue a delivery receipt identifying the parcel received and confirming the date it was received and the person who presented it.

2) The Registry Officer will in due course verify:

a) that the claim has been submitted by a person or body who, in accordance with the decisions of the Governing Council, has a right to file claims with the Commission;

b) that the claim has been submitted within the relevant time-limit established by the Governing Council;

c) that, in the case of a corporation or other private legal entity making a claim directly to the Commission in accordance with Article 5, paragraph 3, above:

i) evidence is attached indicating that a request was made by the entity concerned to the State of its incorporation or organization to submit its claim to the Commission;

ii) explanation is provided as to why the claim was not submitted by a Government.

Article 12. <u>Unauthorized or Late Submissions</u>

1) In the case of claims submitted by an unauthorized person or entity, including claims presented by a corporation or other private legal entity without showing that a previous request has been made to the State of its incorporation or organization, the Executive Secretary will return the documents received, and inform the person or entity concerned of the reasons why the claim cannot be registered.

2) In the case of claims submitted by an authorized person or body after the expiration of the time-limit set by the Governing Council for a given category of claims,the Executive Secretary will report to the Governing Council. The Governing Council will decide whether to accept the late-filed claims or not.

Article 13. Filing Receipt

If the claim is submitted by an authorized person or body within the established time-limit, the Registry Officer will register the claim and issue a filing receipt indicating:

a) the claim and its category;
b) the party who presented the claim;
c) the number of claims contained in a consolidated claim;
d) the number assigned to the claim for identification.

Article 14. Preliminary Assessment

1) The Secretariat will make a preliminary assessment of the claims received in order to determine whether they meet the formal requirements established by the Governing Council. To this end the Secretariat will verify:

a) that the claims have been submitted on the appropriate claim forms with the required number of copies, and in English or with an English translation;

b) that the claims contain the names and addresses of the claimants and, where applicable, evidence of the amount, type and causes of losses;

c) that the affirmation by the Government has been included in respect of each consolidated claim stating that, to the best of the information available to it, the claimants are its nationals or residents, and that it has no reason to believe that the information stated in the claims is incorrect;

d) that all required affirmations have been given by each claimant.

2) In the case of claims of corporations and other legal entities the Secretariat will also verify that each separate claim contains:

a) documents evidencing the name, address and place of incorporation or organization of the entity;

b) evidence that the corporation or the legal entity was, on the date on which the claim arose, incorporated or organized under the law of the State the Government of which has submitted the claim;

c) a general description of the legal structure of the entity;

d) an affirmation by the authorized official for each corporation or other entity that the information contained in the claim is correct.

Article 15. Claims Not Meeting the Formal Requirements

If it is found that the claim does not meet the formal requirements established by the Governing Council, the Secretariat will notify the person or body that submitted the claim about that circumstance and will give it 60 days from the date of that notification to remedy the defect. If the formal requirements are not met within this period, the claim shall not be considered as filed.

Article 16. Reports and Views on Claims

1) The Executive Secretary will make periodic reports to the Governing Council concerning claims received. These reports shall be made as frequently as required to inform the Council of the Commission's case load but not less than quarterly. The reports shall indicate:

a) Governments, international organizations or other eligible parties that have submitted claims;

b) the categories of claims submitted;

c) the number of claimants in each consolidated claim;

d) the total amount of compensation sought in each consolidated claim;

In addition, each report may indicate significant legal and factual issues raised by the claims, if any.

2) The Executive Secretary's report will be promptly circulated to the Government of Iraq as well as to all Governments and international organizations that have submitted claims.

3) Within 30 days in case of claims in Categories A, B and C, and 90 days in case of claims in other categories, of the date of the circulation of the Executive Secretary's report, the Government of Iraq as well as Governments and international organizations that have submitted claims, may present their additional information and views concerning the report to the Executive Secretary for transmission to panels of Commissioners in accordance with Article 32. There shall be no extensions of the time-limits specified in this paragraph.

4) Requirements set forth in Articles 3, 4, 6 (3), 7, 8 and 11 (1) shall apply to such additional information and views.

Article 17. <u>Categorization of Claims</u>

In order to facilitate the work of Commissioners and to ensure uniformity in the treatment of similar claims, the Secretariat will proceed to categorize claims according to, <u>inter</u> <u>alia</u>, the type or size of the claims and the similarity of legal and factual issues.

III) COMMISSIONERS

Article 18. Appointment

1) Commissioners shall be appointed for specific tasks and terms by the Governing Council upon nomination by the Secretary-General on the basis of recommendations of the Executive Secretary.

2) The Secretary-General has established a Register of Experts which, as stated in his 12 June 1991 invitation for the submission of names of experts, while not limiting his selection, might be drawn upon when Commissioners are nominated for appointment. The Executive Secretary will keep and up-date the register.

Article 19. Qualifications

1) In nominating and appointing the Commissioners, due regard shall be paid to the need for geographical representation, professional qualifications, experience and integrity.

2) Commissioners will be experts in fields such as finance, law, accounting, insurance, environmental damage assessment, oil, trade and engineering.

3) Nominations and appointments of Commissioners shall be made paying due regard to the nature of the claims and categories of claims to be assigned to them.

Article 20. Procedure for Appointment

1) The Executive Secretary will transmit to the Governing Council the nominations for Commissioners proposed by the Secretary-General, indicating which Commissioners are to serve on each panel and who, within each panel, will act as a Chairman.

2) The Executive Secretary will recommend to the Secretary-General for nomination as many panels of Commissioners as necessary to process claims in an expeditious manner.

3) When transmitting to the Governing Council the nominations for Commissioners, the Executive Secretary will specify the claims or categories of claims to be assigned to each panel, indicating the expertise and the number of Commissioners required.

4) If the Governing Council does not agree on the appointment of a nominee for a panel, it will request the Secretary-General, through the Executive Secretary, to submit a new nomination.

5) If, at the time the Executive Secretary transmits the new nomination, the Governing Council is not in session, the new nomination will be communicated to the members of the Governing Council. The Governing Council may approve replacement Commissioners at intersessional meetings.

6) The same procedure will apply whenever a new Commissioner must be nominated.

Article 21. Requirements

1) Commissioners will act in their personal capacity. Commissioners shall not have financial interests in any of the claims submitted to them or to the panel to which they belong. They may not be associated with or have financial interests in any corporations whose claims have been submitted to them or to the panel to which they belong.

2) Commissioners shall not represent or advise any party or claimant concerning the preparation or presentation of their claims to the Commission during their service as Commissioner or for two years thereafter.

Article 22. Disclosure

1) All prospective Commissioners shall file a statement that shall disclose to the Executive Secretary any prior or actual relationship with Governments, corporations or individuals, or any other circumstances, that are likely to give rise to justifiable doubts as to his impartiality or independence with respect to his prospective tasks. This information will be provided to the Governing Council at the time the nomination of the prospective Commissioner is transmitted.

2) A Commissioner, once appointed, shall disclose to the Executive Secretary any new circumstances likely to give rise to justifiable doubts as to his impartiality or independence.

3) When any Commissioner obtains knowledge that any particular claim before his panel involves circumstances likely to give rise to justifiable doubts as to his impartiality or independence with respect to that claim or group of claims, he shall disclose such circumstances to the Executive Secretary and, if appropriate, shall disqualify himself as to that case.

4) If any Government, international organization, individual claimant, or Commissioner becomes aware of circumstances that give rise to justifiable doubts as to a Commissioner's impartiality or independence, such circumstances must be communicated to the Executive Secretary not later than fifteen days after they became known.

5) The Executive Secretary will inform the Governing Council about the circumstances brought to his attention or of which he learns that are likely to give rise to justifiable doubts as to the impartiality or independence of a Commissioner, transmitting a statement of the Commissioner concerned.

6) In any case in which such circumstances are disclosed to the Governing Council, it may determine whether the Commissioner should cease to act, either generally or with respect to a particular claim or claims. Pending such a determination by the Governing Council, the Commissioner concerned will continue to perform his tasks.

Article 23. Resignation

1) A Commissioner who intends to resign from his office shall communicate his decision, through the Executive Secretary, to the Governing Council.

2) A Commissioner who has submitted his resignation shall continue to perform his functions until such time as his resignation is accepted by the Governing Council.

Article 24. Completion of Work

If a Commissioner resigns during the course of consideration of any particular claim or group of claims, the Commissioner will continue to serve for the limited purpose of completing work on that particular claim or group of claims, unless excused by the Governing Council.

Article 25. Failure to Act

In the event that a Commissioner fails to act or in the event of *de jure* or *de facto* impossibility of his performing his functions, the Executive Secretary shall inform the Governing Council, which may decide to replace the Commissioner in accordance with the procedures set forth in Article 20 (6).

Article 26. Privileges and Immunities

Commissioners, when performing functions for the Commission, will have the status of experts on mission within the meaning of Article VI of the Convention on the Privileges and Immunities of the United Nations of February 13, 1946.

Article 27. Declaration

Every Commissioner shall, before taking up his duties, make the following declaration:

> "I solemnly declare that I will perform my duties and exercise my position as Commissioner honourably, faithfully, independently, impartially and conscientiously."

This declaration shall be signed and delivered to the Executive Secretary, and attached to the documents pertaining to the Commissioner's appointment.

IV) PROCEDURES GOVERNING THE WORK OF THE PANELS

Article 28. Constitution of Panels

1) Unless otherwise decided by the Governing Council, Commissioners will work in panels of three members. Each of the members of a panel shall be of different nationality.

2) Priority is to be given to the establishment of panels of Commissioners to deal with claims in categories A, B and C.

Article 29. Organization of Work

Chairmen of the panels will organize the work of their respective panels so as to ensure the expeditious processing of the claims and the consistent application of the relevant criteria and these Rules.

Article 30. Confidentiality

1) Unless otherwise provided in these procedures or decided by the Governing Council, all records received or developed by the Commission will be confidential, but the Secretariat may provide status reports to Governments, international organizations or corporations making claims directly to the Commission in accordance with Article 5, paragraph 3, regarding claims that they have submitted.

2) Panels will conduct their work in private.

3) Commissioners shall not disclose, even after the termination of their functions, any information not in the public domain that has come to their knowledge by reason of their working for the Commission.

Article 31. Applicable Law

In considering the claims, Commissioners will apply Security Council resolution 687 (1991) and other relevant Security Council resolutions, the criteria established by the Governing Council for particular categories of claims, and any pertinent decisions of the Governing Council. In addition, where necessary, Commissioners shall apply other relevant rules of international law.

Article 32. Submission of Claims to Panels

1) Following the appointment of Commissioners by the Governing Council, the Executive Secretary will submit to panels of Commissioners the single claims or categories of claims assigned to each of them together with the related documentation, containing the results of the preliminary assessment made by the Secretariat and any other information deemed to be useful for the work of the Commissioners, as well as the additional information and views submitted in accordance with Article 16.

2) Any information received by the Secretariat after the expiration of the time-limits as established in Article 16 will be submitted when received, but the work of the panel will not be delayed pending receipt or consideration of such information.

3) The Executive Secretary may, after consulting the relevant panel chairmen, reallocate a claim or claims from one panel to another in order to ensure the efficient processing of claims.

Article 33. Work of the Panels

1) After receiving claims from the Executive Secretary, Commissioners will examine them and meet to deliberate and prepare their recommendations to the Governing Council.

2) Panels of Commissioners will normally meet at the headquarters of the Secretariat. Meetings will be held to the extent deemed necessary by the Chairman of each panel. Commissioners will continue their work on the claims while away from the headquarters of the Secretariat, conducting the necessary communications among themselves and with the Secretariat.

3) Any recommendation or other decision of the panel shall be made by a majority of the Commissioners.

Article 34. Assistance by the Executive Secretary

1) The Executive Secretary and the staff of the Secretariat will provide administrative, technical and legal support to the Commissioners, including the development and maintenance of a computerized database for claims and assistance in obtaining additional information.

2) In considering the claims, the Commissioners will take into account the results of the preliminary assessment of claims made by the Secretariat in accordance with Article 14, as well as other information and views that the Executive Secretary may provide in accordance with Article 32.

3) A member of the Secretariat may attend sessions of the panel and may, if required, provide information to the Commissioners.

Article 35. Evidence

1) Each claimant is responsible for submitting documents and other evidence which demonstrate satisfactorily that a particular claim or group of claims is eligible for compensation pursuant to Security Council resolution 687 (1991). Each panel will determine the admissibility, relevance, materiality and weight of any documents and other evidence submitted.

2) With respect to claims received under the Criteria for Expedited Processing of Urgent Claims (S/AC.26/1991/1), the following guidelines will apply:

a) For the payment of fixed amounts in the case of departures, claimants are required to provide simple documentation of the fact and date of departure from Iraq or Kuwait. Documentation of the actual amount of loss will not be required.

b) For the payment of fixed amounts in the case of serious personal injury not resulting in death, claimants are required to provide simple documentation of the fact and date of the injury; in the case of death, claimants are required to provide simple documentation of the death and family relationship. Documentation of the actual amount of loss will not be required.

c) For consideration of claims up to US$ 100,000 of actual losses, such claims must be documented by appropriate evidence of the circumstances and amount of the claimed loss. Documents and other evidence required will be the reasonable minimum that is appropriate under the particular circumstances of the case. A lesser degree of documentary evidence ordinarily will be sufficient for smaller claims such as those below US$ 20,000.

3) With respect to claims received under the Criteria for Processing Claims of Individuals not Otherwise Covered, Claims of Corporations and Other Entities, and Claims of Governments and International Organizations (S/AC.26/1991/7/Rev.1) , such claims must be supported by documentary and other appropriate evidence sufficient to demonstrate the circumstances and amount of the claimed loss.

4) A panel of Commissioners may request evidence required under this Article.

Article 36. Additional Information

A panel of Commissioners may:

a) in unusually large or complex cases, request further written submissions and invite individuals, corporations or other entities, Governments or international organizations to present their views in oral proceedings;

b) request additional information from any other source, including expert advice, as necessary.

Article 37. Review by Commissioners of Urgent Claims

With respect to claims received under the Criteria for Expedited Processing of Urgent claims (S/AC.26/1991/1), the following expedited procedures may be used:

a) The Secretariat will proceed to check individual claims by matching them, insofar as possible, against the information in its computerized database. The results of the database analysis may be cross checked by the panel.

b) With respect to claims that cannot be completely verified through the computerized database, if the volume of claims is large, the panel may check individual claims on the basis of a sampling with further verification only as circumstances warrant.

c) Each panel will make its recommendations on the basis of the documents submitted, taking into account the preliminary assessment conducted in accordance with Article 14, any other information and views submitted in accordance with Article 32 and any information submitted in accordance with Article 34. Each panel will normally make its recommendations without holding an oral proceeding. The panel may determine that special circumstances warrant holding an oral proceeding concerning a particular claim or claims.

d) Each panel will complete its review of the claims assigned to it and issue its report as soon as possible but no later than 120 days from the date the claims in question are submitted to the panel.

e) Each panel will report in writing through the Executive Secretary to the Governing Council on the claims received and the amount recommended to be allocated to each Government or other entity for each consolidated claim. Each report will briefly explain the reasons for the recommendations and, to the extent practicable within the time-limit, contain a breakdown of the recommendations in respect of individual claims within each consolidated claim.

Article 38. Review by Commissioners of Other Claims

With respect to claims received under the Criteria for Processing of Claims of Individuals not Otherwise Covered; Claims of Corporations and Other Entities; and Claims of Governments and International Organizations (S/AC.26/1991/7/Rev.1), the following procedures will be used:

a) In so far as possible, claims with significant common legal and factual issues will be processed together.

b) Panels may adopt special procedures appropriate to the character, amount and subject-matter of the particular types of claims under consideration.

c) Each panel will complete its review of any claim or group of claims and report in writing through the Executive Secretary to the Governing Council within 180 days of the date the claims in question are submitted to the panel, except for any unusually large or complex claims referred for detailed review, as described below. Each panel will make its recommendations on the basis of the documents submitted, taking into account the preliminary assessment conducted in accordance with Article 14, any other information and views submitted in accordance with Article 32 and any information submitted in accordance with Article 34.

d) Unusually large or complex claims may receive detailed review, as appropriate. If so, the panel considering such a claim may, in its discretion, ask for additional written submissions and hold oral proceedings. In such a case, the individual, corporation, Government, international organization or other entity making the claim may present the case directly to the panel, and may be assisted by an attorney or other representative of choice. The panel will complete its review of the case and report in writing through the Executive Secretary its recommendations to the Governing Council within twelve months of the date the claim was submitted to the panel.

e) Each panel will report in writing through the Executive Secretary to the Governing Council on the claims received and the amount recommended to be awarded for each claimant. Each report will briefly explain the reasons for the recommendations.

Article 39. Additional Time

If a panel considering a claim or group of claims cannot complete its work within the allotted time, the panel will notify the Governing Council through the Executive Secretary of the estimated additional time required. The Governing Council will decide whether the panel should continue its work on the claims or group of claims, with a time-limit to be decided by the Council, or should be discharged of the claim or group of claims, which would be given to another panel.

Article 40. Decisions

1) The amounts recommended by the panels of Commissioners will be subject to approval by the Governing Council. The Governing Council may review the amounts recommended and, where it determines circumstances require, increase or reduce them.

2) The Governing Council may, in its discretion, return a particular claim or group of claims for further review by the Commissioners.

3) The Governing Council will make its decisions on amounts to be awarded at each session with respect to claims covered in any reports of Commissioners circulated to members of the Governing Council at least 30 days in advance of the session.

4) Decisions of the Governing Council will be final and are not subject to appeal or review on procedural, substantive or other grounds.

5) Decisions of the Governing Council and, after the relevant decision is made, the associated report of the panel of Commissioners, will be made public, except the Executive Secretary will delete from the reports of panels of Commissioners the identities of individual claimants and other information determined by the panels to be confidential or privileged.

Article 41. Correction of Decisions

1) Computational, clerical, typographical or other errors brought to the attention of the Executive Secretary within 60 days from the publication of the decisions and reports, will be reported by the Executive Secretary to the Governing Council.

2) The Governing Council will decide whether any action is necessary. If it is determined that a correction must be made, the Governing Council will direct the Executive Secretary as to the proper method of correction.

Article 42. Withdrawal of Claims

A claim pending before the Commission may be withdrawn at any time by the Government or entity that submitted the claim to the Commission. In any case where the claim has been paid, settled or otherwise resolved, it shall be withdrawn.

Article 43. Additional Procedural Rulings

Subject to the provisions of these procedures, Commissioners may make such additional procedural rulings as may be necessary to complete work on particular cases or categories of cases. In so doing, the Commissioners may rely on the relevant UNCITRAL Rules for guidance. Commissioners may request the Governing Council to provide further guidance with respect to these procedures at any time. The Governing Council may adopt further procedures or revise these Rules when circumstances warrant.

UNITED NATIONS

S

Security Council

Distr.
GENERAL

S/AC.26/1992/13
25 September 1992

Original: ENGLISH

UNITED NATIONS
COMPENSATION COMMISSION
GOVERNING COUNCIL
Seventh Session
Geneva, 21-25 September 1991

Decision taken by the Governing Council of the United Nations Compensation Commission at its 29th meeting held on 24 September 1992

Further Measures to Avoid Multiple Recovery of Compensation by Claimants

With a view to avoiding multiple recovery of compensation by claimants for the same losses, the Governing Council, in addition to measures already taken:

1. Decides to request the Government of Iraq to provide the Commission with information about claims against Iraq in national courts or other fora for losses that would also be eligible for compensation by the Commission, and about compensation awarded for such losses.

2. Decides to invite Governments to seek to obtain and to provide the Commission with any information regarding:

a. any lawsuit pending in the courts of their jurisdiction against Iraq, or any compensation granted by those courts, for losses resulting from Iraq's invasion and occupation of Kuwait;

b. recipients of payment made or relief provided by the respective Government, Civil I.D. or Residency

GE.92-63105

Permit numbers, passport numbers, dates of birth, types of losses and amounts paid; and

c. recipients of payments made or relief provided by employers known to have operated in Iraq or Kuwait, for losses incurred by their employers as a result of Iraq's invasion and occupation of Kuwait, including where available, their names, Civil I.D. or Residency Permit numbers, passport numbers, dates of birth, types of losses and amounts paid.

3. Noting that, in light of Decision 1 (S/AC.26/1991/1), the questions of multiple recovery and deductions from payments made in respect of claims in categories "A" and "B" do not arise, decides to adopt the following guidelines for the payment of compensation in cases where multiple recovery for the same loss may occur:

a. Governments or employers that seek reimbursement under category "E" or "F" claims of amounts paid for losses that had already been paid from the Fund to individual claimants under categories "C" and "D" claims will not be eligible for compensation. If a request for reimbursement from the Fund is submitted to the Commission by the Government or the employer while the "C" or "D" claim of the individual concerned is being processed before the Commission, the amount of compensation already received by the individual (as shown by the Government or employer) will have to be deducted from his or her claim.

b. When the Commission learns, either through information provided by the claimant or through other means, and before paying compensation from the Fund, that a claimant in categories "C", "D", "E" and "F" has received compensation elsewhere for the same loss, the amount already received will be deducted from the compensation to be paid from the Fund to that claimant for the same loss.

UNITED NATIONS

S

Security Council

Distr.
GENERAL

S/AC.26/Dec.17 (1994) _*/
24 March 1994

Original: ENGLISH

UNITED NATIONS
COMPENSATION COMMISSION
GOVERNING COUNCIL

PRIORITY OF PAYMENT AND PAYMENT MECHANISM
Guiding Principles

Decision taken by the Governing Council of the United Nations Compensation Commission at its 41st meeting, held in Geneva on 23 March 1994

1. In striving to resolve the question of how to allocate the funding available to pay awards to claimants within each category of claims as well as how to allocate available funding among the various categories of claims, Governing Council has been guided by the following basic principles:

A. The Compensation Commission should ensure that similarly situated claimants within each category of claims are treated equally, to the extent feasible, regardless of the chronological order in which their claims are decided;

B. Claimants with claims in the three categories of urgent claims (categories "A", "B" and "C") shall receive priority of treatment, including at both the processing and the payment stages, in accordance with the prior decisions and statements of the Government Council.

Payment Mechanism

2. Payment of an initial amount of US$2,500 (or the principal amount of the award, if less) will be made to each successful claimant in categories "A", "B" and "C".

_*/ Decisions of the Governing Council of the United Nations Compensation Commission are now being issued under the symbol S/AC.26/Dec.

3. Such payments in respect of successful claimants in categories "A"," B" and "C" wi be made by the Compensation Commission to Governments as awards in each category are confirmed by the Governing Council.

4. Such payments will begin when sufficient funds have been accumulated in the Compensation Fund to make payment on all claims approved in the first instalments in categories "A", "B" and "C". Subsequent such payments will also be made when sufficient funds have been accumulated in the Compensation Fund to make payment on all approved claims, within each instalment.

Allocation of Funds

5. For an initial period, successful claimants in categories "A", "B" and "C" will recei all funds available in the Compensation Fund for paying claims, until each has received payment of the initial amount referenced in paragraph 2 above.

6. After the payments in paragraph 2 have been made, the funds available to the Commission for the payment of claims will be allocated as follows:

The Executive Secretary will transfer funds to each appropriate Government in respe of approved claims in all categories. Such transfers will be made when there are funds in th Compensation Fund at least sufficient to make a minimum payment of US$5000 (or the unp principal amount of the award, if less) in respect of each approved claim. Amounts transferred in addition to this minimum of US$5000 payment will be proportional to the rati between the unpaid balance of approved claims submitted by that Government and the unpa balance of all approved claims.

7. The Compensation Commission will retain an adequate operating reserve consisting an amount sufficient to cover at least one year's operating expenses.

Revision of the System

8. The Governing Council will monitor the payment system and make revisions wherev and whenever needed in order that the mechanism may evolve and adjust to ongoing circumstances, including the amounts available in the Fund for the payment of claims.

9. If there are insufficient funds to make payments in accordance with the mechanism outlined above, the Governing Council, keeping in mind the principles stated in paragraph above, may decide on how to distribute any limited funds available. In particular, this shou not exclude the possibility of distributing the amounts stated in paragraphs 2 and 6 above by successive payments.

Transparency

10. Distribution of compensation will be the responsibility of each Government concerne

-----

UNITED NATIONS **S**

Security Council

Distr.
GENERAL

S/AC.26/Dec.19 (1994)
24 March 1994

Original: ENGLISH

UNITED NATIONS
COMPENSATION COMMISSION
GOVERNING COUNCIL

MILITARY COSTS

Decision taken by the Governing Council of the United Nations Compensation Commission at its 41st meeting, held in Geneva on 24 March 1994

The Governing Council confirms that the costs of the Allied Coalition Forces, including those of military operations against Iraq, are not eligible for compensation.

ANNEX III

The General Framework Agreement for Peace in Bosnia and Herzegovina

Initialled in Dayton on 21 November 1995
and signed in Paris on 14 December 1995

The Republic of Bosnia and Herzegovina, the Republic of Croatia and the Federal Republic of Yugoslavia (the "Parties"),

Recognizing the need for a comprehensive settlement to bring an end to the tragic conflict in the region,

Desiring to contribute toward that end and to promote an enduring peace and stability,

Affirming their commitment to the Agreed Basic Principles issued on September 8, 1995, the Further Agreed Basic Principles issued on September 26, 1995, and the cease-fire agreements of September 14 and October 5, 1995,

Noting the agreement of August 29, 1995, which authorized the delegation of the Federal Republic of Yugoslavia to sign, on behalf of the Republika Srpska, the parts of the peace plan concerning it, with the obligation to implement the agreement that is reached strictly and consequently,

Have agreed as follows:

Article I

The Parties shall conduct their relations in accordance with the principles set forth in the United Nations Charter, as well as the Helsinki Final Act and other documents of the Organization for Security and Cooperation in Europe. In particular, the Parties shall fully respect the sovereign equality of one another, shall settle disputes by peaceful means, and shall refrain from any action, by threat or use of force or otherwise, against the territorial integrity or political independence of Bosnia and Herzegovina or any other State.

Article II

The Parties welcome and endorse the arrangements that have been made concerning the military aspects of the peace settlement and aspects of regional stabilization, as set forth in the Agreements at Annex 1-A and Annex 1-B. The Parties shall fully respect and promote fulfillment of the commitments made in Annex 1-A, and shall comply fully with their commitments as set forth in Annex 1-B.

Article III

The Parties welcome and endorse the arrangements that have been made concerning the boundary demarcation between the two Entities, the Federation of Bosnia and Herzegovina and Republika Srpska, as set forth in the Agreement at Annex 2. The Parties shall fully respect and promote fulfillment of the commitments made therein.

Article IV

The Parties welcome and endorse the elections program for Bosnia and Herzegovina as set forth in Annex 3. The Parties shall fully respect and promote fulfillment of that program.

Article V

The Parties welcome and endorse the arrangements that have been made concerning the Constitution of Bosnia and Herzegovina, as set forth in Annex 4. The Parties shall fully respect and promote fulfillment of the commitments made therein.

Article VI

The Parties welcome and endorse the arrangements that have been made concerning the establishment of an arbitration tribunal, a Commission on Human Rights, a Commission on Refugees and Displaced Persons, a Commission to Preserve National Monuments, and Bosnia and Herzegovina Public Corporations, as set forth in the Agreements at Annexes 5-9. The Parties shall fully respect and promote fulfillment of the commitments made therein.

Article VII

Recognizing that the observance of human rights and the protection of refugees and displaced persons are of vital importance in achieving a lasting peace, the Parties agree to and shall comply fully with the provisions concerning human rights set forth in Chapter One of the Agreement at Annex 6, as well as the provisions concerning refugees and displaced persons set forth in Chapter One of the Agreement at Annex 7.

Article VIII

The Parties welcome and endorse the arrangements that have been made concerning the implementation of this peace settlement, including in particular those pertaining to the civilian (non-military) implementation, as set forth in the Agreement at Annex 10, and the international police task force, as set forth in the Agreement at Annex 11. The Parties shall fully respect and promote fulfillment of the commitments made therein.

Article IX

The Parties shall cooperate fully with all entities involved in implementation of this peace settlement, as described in the Annexes to this Agreement, or which are otherwise authorized by the United Nations Security Council, pursuant to the obligation of all Parties to cooperate in the investigation and prosecution of war crimes and other violations of international humanitarian law.

Article X

The Federal Republic of Yugoslavia and the Republic of Bosnia and Herzegovina recognize each other as sovereign independent States within their international borders. Further aspects of their mutual recognition will be subject to subsequent discussions.

Article XI

This Agreement shall enter into force upon signature.

DONE at Paris, this 14 day of December, 1995, in the Bosnian, Croatian, English and Serbian languages, each text being equally authentic.

For the Republic of Bosnia and Herzegovina
For the Republic of Croatia
For the Federal Republic of Yugoslavia

Witnessed by:

European Union Special Negotiator
For the French Republic
For the Federal Republic of Germany

For the Russian Federation
For the United Kingdom of Great Britain and Northern Ireland
For the United States of America

Annexes[1]

Annex 1-A: Agreement on Military Aspects of the Peace Settlement
Annex 1-B: Agreement on Regional Stabilization
Annex 2: Agreement on Inter-Entity Boundary Line and Related Issues
Annex 3: Agreement on Elections
Annex 4: Constitution
Annex 5: Agreement on Arbitration
Annex 6: Agreement on Human Rights
Annex 7: Agreement on Refugees and Displaced Persons
Annex 8: Agreement on the Commission to Preserve National Monuments
Annex 9: Agreement on Bosnia and Herzegovina Public Corporations
Annex 10: Agreement on Civilian Implementation
Annex 11: Agreement on International Police Task Force

Office of the High Representative

1. *Editorial Note:* Only Annexes 5, 6, 7 and 10 are reproduced here.

Annex 5: Agreement on Arbitration

The Federation of Bosnia and Herzegovina and the Republika Srpska agree to honor the following obligations as set forth in the Agreed Basic Principles adopted at Geneva on September 8, 1995, by the Republic of Bosnia and Herzegovina, the Republic of Croatia, and the Federal Republic of Yugoslavia, the latter representing also the Republika Srpska:

Paragraph 2.4

"The two entities will enter into reciprocal commitments

. . .

(c) to engage in binding arbitration to resolve disputes between them."

Paragraph 3

"The entities have agreed in principle to the following:

. . .

3.5 The design and implementation of a system of arbitration for the solution of disputes between the two entities."

For the Federation of Bosnia and Herzegovina
For the Republika Srpska

Office of the High Representative

Annex 6: Agreement on Human Rights

The Republic of Bosnia and Herzegovina, the Federation of Bosnia and Herzegovina and the Republika Srpska (the "Parties") have agreed as follows:

CHAPTER ONE. RESPECT FOR HUMAN RIGHTS

Article I. Fundamental Rights and Freedoms

The Parties shall secure to all persons within their jurisdiction the highest level of internationally recognized human rights and fundamental freedoms, including the rights and freedoms provided in the European Convention for the Protection of Human Rights and Fundamental Freedoms and its Protocols and the other international agreements listed in the Appendix to this Annex. These include:

1. The right to life.

2. The right not to be subjected to torture or to inhuman or degrading treatment or punishment.

3. The right not to be held in slavery or servitude or to perform forced or compulsory labor.

4. The rights to liberty and security of person.

5. The right to a fair hearing in civil and criminal matters, and other rights relating to criminal proceedings.

6. The right to private and family life, home, and correspondence.

7. Freedom of thought, conscience and religion.

8. Freedom of expression.

9. Freedom of peaceful assembly and freedom of association with others.

10. The right to marry and to found a family.

11. The right to property.

12. The right to education.

13. The right to liberty of movement and residence.

14. The enjoyment of the rights and freedoms provided for in this Article or in the international agreements listed in the Annex to this Constitution secured without discrimination on any ground such as sex, race, color, language, religion, political or other opinion, national or social origin, association with a national minority, property, birth or other status.

CHAPTER TWO. THE COMMISSION ON HUMAN RIGHTS

Part A. General

Article II. Establishment of the Commission

1. To assist in honoring their obligations under this Agreement, the Parties hereby establish a Commission on Human Rights (the "Commission"). The Commission shall consist of two parts: the Office of the Ombudsman and the Human Rights Chamber.

2. The Office of the Ombudsman and the Human Rights Chamber shall consider, as subsequently described:

a. alleged or apparent violations of human rights as provided in the European Convention for the Protection of Human Rights and Fundamental Freedoms and the Protocols thereto, or

b. alleged or apparent discrimination on any ground such as sex, race, color, language, religion, political or other opinion, national or social origin, association with a national minority, property, birth or other status arising in the enjoyment of any of the rights and freedoms provided for in the international agreements listed in the Appendix to this Annex, where such violation is alleged or appears to have been committed by the Parties, including by any official or organ of the Parties, Cantons, Municipalities, or any individual acting under the authority of such official or organ.

3. The Parties recognize the right of all persons to submit to the Commission and to other human rights bodies applications concerning alleged violations of human rights, in accordance with the procedures of this Annex and such bodies. The Parties shall not undertake any punitive action directed against persons who intend to submit, or have submitted, such allegations.

Article III. Facilities, Staff and Expenses

1. The Commission shall have appropriate facilities and a professionally competent staff. There shall be an Executive Officer, appointed jointly by the Ombudsman and the President of the Chamber, who shall be responsible for all necessary administrative arrangements with respect to facilities and staff. The Executive Officer shall be subject to the direction of the Ombudsman and the President of the Chamber insofar as concerns their respective administrative and professional office staff.

2. The salaries and expenses of the Commission and its staff shall be determined jointly by the Parties and shall be borne by Bosnia and Herzegovina. The salaries and expenses shall be fully adequate to implement the Commission's mandate.

3. The Commission shall have its headquarters in Sarajevo, including both the headquarters Office of the Ombudsman and the facilities for the Chamber. The Ombudsman shall have at least one additional office in the territory of the Federation and the Republika Srpska and at other locations as it deems appropriate. The Chamber may meet in other locations where it determines that the needs of a particular case so require, and may meet at any place it deems appropriate for the inspection of property, documents or other items.

4. The Ombudsman and all members of the Chamber shall not be held criminally or civilly liable for any acts carried out within the scope of their duties. When the Ombudsman and members of the Chamber are not citizens of Bosnia and Herzegovina, they and their families shall be accorded the same privileges and immunities as are enjoyed by diplomatic agents and their families under the Vienna Convention on Diplomatic Relations.

5. With full regard for the need to maintain impartiality, the Commission may receive assistance as it deems appropriate from any governmental, international, or non-governmental organization.

Part B. Human Rights Ombudsman

Article IV. Human Rights Ombudsman

1. The Parties hereby establish the Office of the Human Rights Ombudsman (the "Ombudsman").

2. The Ombudsman shall be appointed for a non-renewable term of five years by the Chairman-in-Office of the Organization for Security and Cooperation in Europe (OSCE), after consultation with the Parties. He or she shall be independently responsible for choosing his or her own staff. Until the transfer described in Article

XIV below, the Ombudsman may not be a citizen of Bosnia and Herzegovina or of any neighboring state. The Ombudsman appointed after that transfer shall be appointed by the Presidency of Bosnia and Herzegovina.

3. Members of the Office of the Ombudsman must be of recognized high moral standing and have competence in the field of international human rights.

4. The Office of the Ombudsman shall be an independent agency. In carrying out its mandate, no person or organ of the Parties may interfere with its functions.

Article V. Jurisdiction of the Ombudsman

1. Allegations of violations of human rights received by the Commission shall generally be directed to the Office of the Ombudsman, except where an applicant specifies the Chamber.

2. The Ombudsman may investigate, either on his or her own initiative or in response to an allegation by any Party or person, non-governmental organization, or group of individuals claiming to be the victim of a violation by any Party or acting on behalf of alleged victims who are deceased or missing, alleged or apparent violations of human rights within the scope of paragraph 2 of Article II. The Parties undertake not to hinder in any way the effective exercise of this right.

3. The Ombudsman shall determine which allegations warrant investigation and in what priority, giving particular priority to allegations of especially severe or systematic violations and those founded on alleged discrimination on prohibited grounds.

4. The Ombudsman shall issue findings and conclusions promptly after concluding an investigation. A Party identified as violating human rights shall, within a specified period, explain in writing how it will comply with the conclusions.

5. Where an allegation is received which is within the jurisdiction of the Human Rights Chamber, the Ombudsman may refer the allegation to the Chamber at any stage.

6. The Ombudsman may also present special reports at any time to any competent government organ or official. Those receiving such reports shall reply within a time limit specified by the Ombudsman, including specific responses to any conclusions offered by the Ombudsman.

7. The Ombudsman shall publish a report, which, in the event that a person or entity does not comply with his or her conclusions and recommendations, will be forwarded to the High Representative described in Annex 10 to the General Framework

Agreement while such office exists, as well as referred for further action to the Presidency of the appropriate Party. The Ombudsman may also initiate proceedings before the Human Rights Chamber based on such Report. The Ombudsman may also intervene in any proceedings before the Chamber.

Article VI. Powers

1. The Ombudsman shall have access to and may examine all official documents, including classified ones, as well as judicial and administrative files, and can require any person, including a government official, to cooperate by providing relevant information, documents and files. The Ombudsman may attend administrative hearings and meetings of other organs and may enter and inspect any place where persons deprived of their liberty are confined or work.

2. The Ombudsman and staff are required to maintain the confidentiality of all confidential information obtained, except where required by order of the Chamber, and shall treat all documents and files in accordance with applicable rules.

Part C. Human Rights Chamber

Article VII. Human Rights Chamber

1. The Human Rights Chamber shall be composed of fourteen members.

2. Within 90 days after this Agreement enters into force, the Federation of Bosnia and Herzegovina shall appoint four members and the Republika Srpska shall appoint two members. The Committee of Ministers of the Council of Europe, pursuant to its resolution (93)6, after consultation with the Parties, shall appoint the remaining members, who shall not be citizens of Bosnia and Herzegovina or any neighboring state, and shall designate one such member as the President of the Chamber.

3. All members of the Chamber shall possess the qualifications required for appointment to high judicial office or be jurists of recognized competence. The members of the Chamber shall be appointed for a term of five years and may be reappointed.

4. Members appointed after the transfer described in Article XIV below shall be appointed by the Presidency of Bosnia and Herzegovina.

Article VIII. Jurisdiction of the Chamber

1. The Chamber shall receive by referral from the Ombudsman on behalf of an applicant, or directly from any Party or person, non-governmental organization, or

group of individuals claiming to be the victim of a violation by any Party or acting on behalf of alleged victims who are deceased or missing, for resolution or decision applications concerning alleged or apparent violations of human rights within the scope of paragraph 2 of Article II.

2. The Chamber shall decide which applications to accept and in what priority to address them. In so doing, the Chamber shall take into account the following criteria:

a. Whether effective remedies exist, and the applicant has demonstrated that they have been exhausted and that the application has been filed with the Commission within six months from such date on which the final decision was taken.

b. The Chamber shall not address any application which is substantially the same as a matter which has already been examined by the Chamber or has already been submitted to another procedure or international investigation or settlement.

c. The Chamber shall also dismiss any application which it considers incompatible with this Agreement, manifestly ill-founded, or an abuse of the right of petition.

d. The Chamber may reject or defer further consideration if the application concerns a matter currently pending before any other international human rights body responsible for the adjudication of applications or the decision of cases, or any other Commission established by the Annexes to the General Framework Agreement.

e. In principle, the Chamber shall endeavor to accept and to give particular priority to allegations of especially severe or systematic violations and those founded on alleged discrimination on prohibited grounds.

f. Applications which entail requests for provisional measures shall be reviewed as a matter of priority in order to determine (1) whether they should be accepted and, if so (2) whether high priority for the scheduling of proceedings on the provisional measures request is warranted.

3. The Chamber may decide at any point in its proceedings to suspend consideration of, reject or strike out, an application on the ground that (a) the applicant does not intend to pursue his application; (b) the matter has been resolved; or (c) for any other reason established by the Chamber, it is no longer justified to continue the examination of the application; provided that such result is consistent with the objective of respect for human rights.

Article IX. Friendly Settlement

1. At the outset of a case or at any stage during the proceedings, the Chamber may attempt to facilitate an amicable resolution of the matter on the basis of respect for the rights and freedoms referred to in this Agreement.

2. If the Chamber succeeds in effecting such a resolution it shall publish a Report and forward it to the High Representative described in Annex 10 to the General Framework Agreement while such office exists, the OSCE and the Secretary General of the Council of Europe. Such a Report shall include a brief statement of the facts and the resolution reached. The report of a resolution in a given case may, however, be confidential in whole or in part where necessary for the protection of human rights or with the agreement of the Chamber and the parties concerned.

Article X. Proceedings before the Chamber

1. The Chamber shall develop fair and effective procedures for the adjudication of applications. Such procedures shall provide for appropriate written pleadings and, on the decision of the Chamber, a hearing for oral argument or the presentation of evidence. The Chamber shall have the power to order provisional measures, to appoint experts, and to compel the production of witnesses and evidence.

2. The Chamber shall normally sit in panels of seven, composed of two members from the Federation, one from the Republika Srpska, and four who are not citizens of Bosnia and Herzegovina or any neighboring state. When an application is decided by a panel, the full Chamber may decide, upon motion of a party to the case or the Ombudsman, to review the decision; such review may include the taking of additional evidence where the Chamber so decides. References in this Annex to the Chamber shall include, as appropriate, the Panel, except that the power to develop general rules, regulations and procedures is vested in the Chamber as a whole.

3. Except in exceptional circumstances in accordance with rules, hearings of the Chamber shall be held in public.

4. Applicants may be represented in proceedings by attorneys or other representatives of their choice, but shall also be personally present unless excused by the Chamber on account of hardship, impossibility, or other good cause.

5. The Parties undertake to provide all relevant information to, and to cooperate fully with, the Chamber.

Article XI. Decisions

1. Following the conclusion of the proceedings, the chamber shall promptly issue a decision, which shall address:

a. whether the facts found indicate a breach by the Party concerned of its obligations under this Agreement; and if so

b. what steps shall be taken by the Party to remedy such breach, including orders to cease and desist, monetary relief (including pecuniary and non-pecuniary injuries), and provisional measures.

2. The Chamber shall make its decision by a majority of members. In the event a decision by the full Chamber results in a tie, the President of the Chamber shall cast the deciding vote.

3. Subject to review as provided in paragraph 2 of Article X, the decisions of the Chamber shall be final and binding.

4. Any member shall be entitled to issue a separate opinion on any case.

5. The Chamber shall issue reasons for its decisions. Its decisions shall be published and forwarded to the parties concerned, the High Representative described in Annex 10 to the General Framework Agreement while such office exists, the Secretary General of the Council of Europe and the OSCE.

6. The Parties shall implement fully decisions of the Chamber.

Article XII. Rules and Regulations

The Chamber shall promulgate such rules and regulations, consistent with this Agreement, as may be necessary to carry out its functions, including provisions for preliminary hearings, expedited decisions on provisional measures, decisions by panels of the Chamber, and review of decisions made by any such panels.

CHAPTER THREE. GENERAL PROVISIONS

Article XIII. Organizations Concerned with Human Rights

1. The Parties shall promote and encourage the activities of non-governmental and international organizations for the protection and promotion of human rights.

2. The Parties join in inviting the United Nations Commission on Human Rights, the OSCE, the United Nations High Commissioner for Human Rights, and other intergovernmental or regional human rights missions or organizations to monitor closely the human rights situation in Bosnia and Herzegovina, including through the establishment of local offices and the assignment of observers, rapporteurs, or other relevant persons on a permanent or mission-by-mission basis and to provide them with full and effective facilitation, assistance and access.

3. The Parties shall allow full and effective access to non-governmental organizations for purposes of investigating and monitoring human rights conditions in Bosnia and Herzegovina and shall refrain from hindering or impeding them in the exercise of these functions.

4. All competent authorities in Bosnia and Herzegovina shall cooperate with and provide unrestricted access to the organizations established in this Agreement; any international human rights monitoring mechanisms established for Bosnia and Herzegovina; the supervisory bodies established by any of the international agreements listed in the Appendix to this Annex; the International Tribunal for the Former Yugoslavia; and any other organization authorized by the U.N. Security Council with a mandate concerning human rights or humanitarian law.

Article XIV. Transfer

Five years after this Agreement enters into force, the responsibility for the continued operation of the Commission shall transfer from the Parties to the institutions of Bosnia and Herzegovina, unless the Parties otherwise agree. In the latter case, the Commission shall continue to operate as provided above.

Article XV. Notice

The Parties shall give effective notice of the terms of this Agreement throughout Bosnia and Herzegovina.

Article XVI. Entry into Force

This Agreement shall enter into force upon signature.

For the Republic of Bosnia and Herzegovina
For the Federation of Bosnia and Herzegovina
For the Republika Srpska

Appendix: Human Rights Agreements

1. 1948 Convention on the Prevention and Punishment of the Crime of Genocide

2. 1949 Geneva Conventions I-IV on the Protection of the Victims of War, and the 1977 Geneva Protocols I-II thereto

3. 1950 European Convention for the Protection of Human Rights and Fundamental Freedoms, and the Protocols thereto

4. 1951 Convention relating to the Status of Refugees and the 1966 Protocol thereto

5. 1957 Convention on the Nationality of Married Women

6. 1961 Convention on the Reduction of Statelessness

7. 1965 International Convention on the Elimination of All Forms of Racial Discrimination

8. 1966 International Covenant on Civil and Political Rights and the 1966 and 1989 Optional Protocols thereto

9. 1966 Covenant on Economic, Social and Cultural Rights

10. 1979 Convention on the Elimination of All Forms of Discrimination against Women

11. 1984 Convention against Torture and Other Cruel, Inhuman or Degrading Treatment or Punishment

12. 1987 European Convention on the Prevention of Torture and Inhuman or Degrading Treatment or Punishment

13. 1989 Convention on the Rights of the Child

14. 1990 Convention on the Protection of the Rights of All Migrant Workers and Members of Their Families

15. 1992 European Charter for Regional or Minority Languages

16. 1994 Framework Convention for the Protection of National Minorities

---

Office of the High Representative

Annex 7: Agreement on Refugees and Displaced Persons

The Republic of Bosnia and Herzegovina, the Federation of Bosnia and Herzegovina, and the Republika Srpska (the "Parties") have agreed as follows:

CHAPTER ONE. PROTECTION

Article I. Rights of Refugees and Displaced Persons

1. All refugees and displaced persons have the right freely to return to their homes of origin. They shall have the right to have restored to them property of which they were deprived in the course of hostilities since 1991 and to be compensated for any property that cannot be restored to them. The early return of refugees and displaced persons is an important objective of the settlement of the conflict in Bosnia and Herzegovina. The Parties confirm that they will accept the return of such persons who have left their territory, including those who have been accorded temporary protection by third countries.

2. The Parties shall ensure that refugees and displaced persons are permitted to return in safety, without risk of harassment, intimidation, persecution, or discrimination, particularly on account of their ethnic origin, religious belief, or political opinion.

3. The Parties shall take all necessary steps to prevent activities within their territories which would hinder or impede the safe and voluntary return of refugees and displaced persons. To demonstrate their commitment to securing full respect for the human rights and fundamental freedoms of all persons within their jurisdiction and creating without delay conditions suitable for return of refugees and displaced persons, the Parties shall take immediately the following confidence building measures:

a. the repeal of domestic legislation and administrative practices with discriminatory intent or effect;

b. the prevention and prompt suppression of any written or verbal incitement, through media or otherwise, of ethnic or religious hostility or hatred;

c. the dissemination, through the media, of warnings against, and the prompt suppression of, acts of retribution by military, paramilitary, and police services, and by other public officials or private individuals;

d. the protection of ethnic and/or minority populations wherever they are found and the provision of immediate access to these populations by international humanitarian organizations and monitors;

e. the prosecution, dismissal or transfer, as appropriate, of persons in military, paramilitary, and police forces, and other public servants, responsible for serious violations of the basic rights of persons belonging to ethnic or minority groups.

4. Choice of destination shall be up to the individual or family, and the principle of the unity of the family shall be preserved. The Parties shall not interfere with the returnees' choice of destination, nor shall they compel them to remain in or move to situations of serious danger or insecurity, or to areas lacking in the basic infrastructure necessary to resume a normal life. The Parties shall facilitate the flow of information necessary for refugees and displaced persons to make informed judgments about local conditions for return.

5. The Parties call upon the United Nations High Commissioner for Refugees ("UNHCR") to develop in close consultation with asylum countries and the Parties a repatriation plan that will allow for an early, peaceful, orderly and phased return of refugees and displaced persons, which may include priorities for certain areas and certain categories of returnees. The Parties agree to implement such a plan and to conform their international agreements and internal laws to it. They accordingly call upon States that have accepted refugees to promote the early return of refugees consistent with international law.

Article II. Creation of Suitable Conditions for Return

1. The Parties undertake to create in their territories the political, economic, and social conditions conducive to the voluntary return and harmonious reintegration of refugees and displaced persons, without preference for any particular group. The Parties shall provide all possible assistance to refugees and displaced persons and work to facilitate their voluntary return in a peaceful, orderly and phased manner, in accordance with the UNHCR repatriation plan.

2. The Parties shall not discriminate against returning refugees and displaced persons with respect to conscription into military service, and shall give positive consideration to requests for exemption from military or other obligatory service based on individual circumstances, so as to enable returnees to rebuild their lives.

Article III. Cooperation with International Organizations and International Monitoring

1. The Parties note with satisfaction the leading humanitarian role of UNHCR, which has been entrusted by the Secretary-General of the United Nations with the role of coordinating among all agencies assisting with the repatriation and relief of refugees and displaced persons.

2. The Parties shall give full and unrestricted access by UNHCR, the International Committee of the Red Cross ("ICRC"), the United Nations Development Programme ("UNDP"), and other relevant international, domestic and nongovernmental organizations to all refugees and displaced persons, with a view to facilitating the work of those organizations in tracing persons, the provision of medical assistance, food distribution, reintegration assistance, the provision of temporary and permanent housing, and other activities vital to the discharge of their mandates and operational responsibilities without administrative impediments. These activities shall include traditional protection functions and the monitoring of basic human rights and humanitarian conditions, as well as the implementation of the provisions of this Chapter.

3. The Parties shall provide for the security of all personnel of such organizations.

Article IV. Repatriation Assistance

The Parties shall facilitate the provision of adequately monitored, short-term repatriation assistance on a nondiscriminatory basis to all returning refugees and displaced persons who are in need, in accordance with a plan developed by UNHCR and other relevant organizations, to enable the families and individuals returning to reestablish their lives and livelihoods in local communities.

Article V. Persons Unaccounted For

The Parties shall provide information through the tracing mechanisms of the ICRC on all persons unaccounted for. The Parties shall also cooperate fully with the ICRC in its efforts to determine the identities, whereabouts and fate of the unaccounted for.

Article VI. Amnesty

Any returning refugee or displaced person charged with a crime, other than a serious violation of international humanitarian law as defined in the Statute of the International Tribunal for the Former Yugoslavia since January 1, 1991 or a common crime unrelated to the conflict, shall upon return enjoy an amnesty. In no case shall charges for crimes be imposed for political or other inappropriate reasons or to circumvent the application of the amnesty.

CHAPTER TWO. COMMISSION FOR DISPLACED PERSONS AND REFUGEES

Article VII. Establishment of the Commission

The Parties hereby establish an independent Commission for Displaced Persons and Refugees (the "Commission"). The Commission shall have its headquarters in Sarajevo and may have offices at other locations as it deems appropriate.

Article VIII. Cooperation

The Parties shall cooperate with the work of the Commission, and shall respect and implement its decisions expeditiously and in good faith, in cooperation with relevant international and nongovernmental organizations having responsibility for the return and reintegration of refugees and displaced persons.

Article IX. Composition

1. The Commission shall be composed of nine members. Within 90 days after this Agreement enters into force, the Federation of Bosnia and Herzegovina shall appoint four members, two for a term of three years and the others for a term of four years, and the Republika Srpska shall appoint two members, one for a term of three years and the other for a term of four years. The President of the European Court of Human Rights shall appoint the remaining members, each for a term of five years, and shall designate one such member as the Chairman. The members of the Commission may be reappointed.

2. Members of the Commission must be of recognized high moral standing.

3. The Commission may sit in panels, as provided in its rules and regulations. References in this Annex to the Commission shall include, as appropriate, such panels, except that the power to promulgate rules and regulations is vested only in the Commission as a whole.

4. Members appointed after the transfer described in Article XVI below shall be appointed by the Presidency of Bosnia and Herzegovina.

Article X. Facilities, Staff and Expenses

1. The Commission shall have appropriate facilities and a professionally competent staff, experienced in administrative, financial, banking and legal matters, to assist it in carrying out its functions. The staff shall be headed by an Executive Officer, who shall be appointed by the Commission.

2. The salaries and expenses of the Commission and its staff shall be determined jointly by the Parties and shall be borne equally by the Parties.

3. Members of the Commission shall not be held criminally or civilly liable for any acts carried out within the scope of their duties. Members of the Commission, and their families, who are not citizens of Bosnia and Herzegovina shall be accorded the same privileges and immunities as are enjoyed by diplomatic agents and their families under the Vienna Convention on Diplomatic Relations.

4. The Commission may receive assistance from international and nongovernmental organizations, in their areas of special expertise falling within the mandate of the Commission, on terms to be agreed.

5. The Commission shall cooperate with other entities established by the General Framework Agreement, agreed by the Parties, or authorized by the United Nations Security Council.

Article XI. Mandate

The Commission shall receive and decide any claims for real property in Bosnia and Herzegovina, where the property has not voluntarily been sold or otherwise transferred since April 1, 1992, and where the claimant does not now enjoy possession of that property. Claims may be for return of the property or for just compensation in lieu of return.

Article XII. Proceedings before the Commission

1. Upon receipt of a claim, the Commission shall determine the lawful owner of the property with respect to which the claim is made and the value of that property. The Commission, through its staff or a duly designated international or nongovernmental organization, shall be entitled to have access to any and all property records in Bosnia and Herzegovina, and to any and all real property located in Bosnia and Herzegovina for purposes of inspection, evaluation and assessment related to consideration of a claim.

2. Any person requesting the return of property who is found by the Commission to be the lawful owner of that property shall be awarded its return. Any person requesting compensation in lieu of return who is found by the Commission to be the lawful owner of that property shall be awarded just compensation as determined by the Commission. The Commission shall make decisions by a majority of its members.

3. In determining the lawful owner of any property, the Commission shall not recognize as valid any illegal property transaction, including any transfer that was made under duress, in exchange for exit permission or documents, or that was otherwise in connection with ethnic cleansing. Any person who is awarded return of property may accept a satisfactory lease arrangement rather than retake possession.

4. The Commission shall establish fixed rates that may be applied to determine the value of all real property in Bosnia and Herzegovina that is the subject of a claim before the Commission. The rates shall be based on an assessment or survey of properties in the territory of Bosnia and Herzegovina undertaken prior to April 1, 1992, if available, or may be based on other reasonable criteria as determined by the Commission.

5. The Commission shall have the power to effect any transactions necessary to transfer or assign title, mortgage, lease, or otherwise dispose of property with respect to which a claim is made, or which is determined to be abandoned. In particular, the Commission may lawfully sell, mortgage, or lease real property to any resident or citizen of Bosnia and Herzegovina, or to either Party, where the lawful owner has sought and received compensation in lieu of return, or where the property is determined to be abandoned in accordance with local law. The Commission may also lease property pending consideration and final determination of ownership.

6. In cases in which the claimant is awarded compensation in lieu of return of the property, the Commission may award a monetary grant or a compensation bond for the future purchase of real property. The Parties welcome the willingness of the international community assisting in the construction and financing of housing in Bosnia and Herzegovina to accept compensation bonds awarded by the Commission as payment, and to award persons holding such compensation bonds priority in obtaining that housing.

7. Commission decisions shall be final, and any title, deed, mortgage, or other legal instrument created or awarded by the Commission shall be recognized as lawful throughout Bosnia and Herzegovina.

8. Failure of any Party or individual to cooperate with the Commission shall not prevent the Commission from making its decision.

Article XIII. Use of Vacant Property

The Parties, after notification to the Commission and in coordination with UNHCR and other international and nongovernmental organizations contributing to relief and reconstruction, may temporarily house refugees and displaced persons in vacant property, subject to final determination of ownership by the Commission and to such temporary lease provisions as it may require.

Article XIV. Refugees and Displaced Persons Property Fund

1. A Refugees and Displaced Persons Property Fund (the "Fund") shall be established in the Central Bank of Bosnia and Herzegovina to be administered by the Commission. The Fund shall be replenished through the purchase, sale, lease and mortgage of real property which is the subject of claims before the Commission. It may also be replenished by direct payments from the Parties, or from contributions by States or international or nongovernmental organizations.

2. Compensation bonds issued pursuant to Article XII(6) shall create future liabilities on the Fund under terms and conditions to be defined by the Commission.

Article XV. Rules and Regulations

The Commission shall promulgate such rules and regulations, consistent with this Agreement, as may be necessary to carry out its functions. In developing these rules and regulations, the Commission shall consider domestic laws on property rights.

Article XVI. Transfer

Five years after this Agreement takes effect, responsibility for the financing and operation of the Commission shall transfer from the Parties to the Government of Bosnia and Herzegovina, unless the Parties otherwise agree. In the latter case, the Commission shall continue to operate as provided above.

Article XVII. Notice

The Parties shall give effective notice of the terms of this Agreement throughout Bosnia and Herzegovina, and in all countries known to have persons who were citizens or residents of Bosnia and Herzegovina.

Article XVIII. Entry into Force

This Agreement shall enter into force upon signature.

For the Republic of Bosnia and Herzegovina
For the Federation of Bosnia and Herzegovina
For the Republika Srpska

Office of the High Representative

Annex 10: Agreement on Civilian Implementation

The Republic of Bosnia and Herzegovina, the Republic of Croatia, the Federal Republic of Yugoslavia, the Federation of Bosnia and Herzegovina, and the Republika Srpska (the "Parties") have agreed as follows:

Article I. High Representative

1. The Parties agree that the implementation of the civilian aspects of the peace settlement will entail a wide range of activities including continuation of the humanitarian aid effort for as long as necessary; rehabilitation of infrastructure and economic reconstruction; the establishment of political and constitutional institutions in Bosnia and Herzegovina; promotion of respect for human rights and the return of displaced persons and refugees; and the holding of free and fair elections according to the timetable in Annex 3 to the General Framework Agreement. A considerable number of international organizations and agencies will be called upon to assist.

2. In view of the complexities facing them, the Parties request the designation of a High Representative, to be appointed consistent with relevant United Nations Security Council resolutions, to facilitate the Parties' own efforts and to mobilize and, as appropriate, coordinate the activities of the organizations and agencies involved in the civilian aspects of the peace settlement by carrying out, as entrusted by a U.N. Security Council resolution, the tasks set out below.

Article II. Mandate and Methods of Coordination and Liaison

1. The High Representative shall:

   a. Monitor the implementation of the peace settlement.

   b. Maintain close contact with the Parties to promote their full compliance with all civilian aspects of the peace settlement and a high level of cooperation between them and the organizations and agencies participating in those aspects.

   c. Coordinate the activities of the civilian organizations and agencies in Bosnia and Herzegovina to ensure the efficient implementation of the civilian aspects of the peace settlement. The High Representative shall respect their autonomy within their spheres of operation while as necessary giving general guidance to them about the impact of their activities on the implementation of the peace settlement. The civilian organizations and agencies are requested to assist the High Representative in the execution of his or her responsibilities by providing all information relevant to their operations in Bosnia-Herzegovina.

d. Facilitate, as the High Representative judges necessary, the resolution of any difficulties arising in connection with civilian implementation.

e. Participate in meetings of donor organizations, particularly on issues of rehabilitation and reconstruction.

f. Report periodically on progress in implementation of the peace agreement concerning the tasks set forth in this Agreement to the United Nations, European Union, United States, Russian Federation, and other interested governments, parties, and organizations.

g. Provide guidance to, and receive reports from, the Commissioner of the International Police Task Force established in Annex 11 to the General Framework Agreement.

2. In pursuit of his or her mandate, the High Representative shall convene and chair a commission (the "Joint Civilian Commission") in Bosnia and Herzegovina. It will comprise senior political representatives of the Parties, the IFOR Commander or his representative, and representatives of those civilian organizations and agencies the High Representative deems necessary.

3. The High Representative shall, as necessary, establish subordinate Joint Civilian Commissions at local levels in Bosnia and Herzegovina.

4. A Joint Consultative Committee will meet from time to time or as agreed between the High Representative and the IFOR Commander.

5. The High Representative or his designated representative shall remain in close contact with the IFOR Commander or his designated representatives and establish appropriate liaison arrangements with the IFOR Commander to facilitate the discharge of their respective responsibilities.

6. The High Representative shall exchange information and maintain liaison on a regular basis with IFOR, as agreed with the IFOR Commander, and through the commissions described in this Article.

7. The High Representative shall attend or be represented at meetings of the Joint Military Commission and offer advice particularly on matters of a political-military nature. Representatives of the High Representative will also attend subordinate

commissions of the Joint Military Commission as set out in Article VIII(8) of Annex 1A to the General Framework Agreement.

8. The High Representative may also establish other civilian commissions within or outside Bosnia and Herzegovina to facilitate the execution of his or her mandate.

9. The High Representative shall have no authority over the IFOR and shall not in any way interfere in the conduct of military operations or the IFOR chain of command.

Article III. Staffing

1. The High Representative shall appoint staff, as he or she deems necessary, to provide assistance in carrying out the tasks herein.

2. The Parties shall facilitate the operations of the High Representative in Bosnia and Herzegovina, including by the provision of appropriate assistance as requested with regard to transportation, subsistence, accommodations, communications, and other facilities at rates equivalent to those provided for the IFOR under applicable agreements.

3. The High Representative shall enjoy, under the laws of Bosnia and Herzegovina, such legal capacity as may be necessary for the exercise of his or her functions, including the capacity to contract and to acquire and dispose of real and personal property.

4. Privileges and immunities shall be accorded as follows:

a. The Parties shall accord the office of the High Representative and its premises, archives, and other property the same privileges and immunities as are enjoyed by a diplomatic mission and its premises, archives, and other property under the Vienna Convention on Diplomatic Relations.

b. The Parties shall accord the High Representative and professional members of his or her staff and their families the same privileges and immunities as are enjoyed by diplomatic agents and their families under the Vienna Convention on Diplomatic Relations.

c. The Parties shall accord other members of the High Representative staff and their families the same privileges and immunities as are enjoyed by members of the administrative and technical staff and their families under the Vienna Convention on Diplomatic Relations.

Article IV. Cooperation

The Parties shall fully cooperate with the High Representative and his or her staff, as well as with the international organizations and agencies as provided for in Article IX of the General Framework Agreement.

Article V. Final Authority to Interpret

The High Representative is the final authority in theater regarding interpretation of this Agreement on the civilian implementation of the peace settlement.

Article VI. Entry into Force

This Agreement shall enter into force upon signature.

For the Republic of Bosnia and Herzegovina
For the Republic of Croatia
For the Federal Republic of Yugoslavia
For the Federation of Bosnia and Herzegovina
For the Republika Srpska

Office of the High Representative